How You Can Be Led
By The Spirit Of God

How You Can Be Led By The Spirit Of God

Kenneth E. Hagin

Second Edition
Seventh Printing 1993

ISBN 0-89276-513-5

In the U.S. write:
Kenneth Hagin Ministries
P.O. Box 50126
Tulsa, OK 74150-0126

In Canada write:
Kenneth Hagin Ministries
P.O. Box 335
Islington (Toronto), Ontario
Canada M9A 4X3

Contents

Preface

In February 1959 in El Paso, Texas, the Lord appeared to me in a vision. He came into my room at 6:30 in the evening, sat down in a chair by my bedside, and talked with me for an hour and a half. I tell more about this in the book, but I want to emphasize something here first.

He talked to me about the ministry of the prophet (Eph. 4:11,12). Then He said, "I did not put prophets in the Church to guide the New Testament Church. My Word says, 'As many as are led by the Spirit of God, they are the sons of God.' Now if you will listen to Me, I am going to teach you how to follow My Spirit. Then I want you to teach My people how to be led by the Spirit."

I am ashamed that I have let many years go by without teaching too much along this line. Occasionally I would get into the edge of it, but I did not really *teach* on it.

So in recent times, the Lord has stirred me up and now I am beginning to teach more on this subject. This book is a part of that stirring.

Chapter 1
The Lamp of the Lord

For as many as are led by the Spirit of God,
they are the sons of God. — Romans 8:14

The Spirit itself [Himself] *beareth witness*
with our spirit, that we are the children of God.
— Romans 8:16

The spirit of man is the candle of the Lord,
searching all the inward parts of the belly.
— Proverbs 20:27

Children of God can expect to be led by the Spirit of God.

Another translation of Proverbs 20:27 reads, "The spirit of man is the *lamp* of the Lord. . . ." Had this verse been written today it might have read, "The spirit of man is the *light bulb* of the Lord." What it means is this: *God will enlighten us — He will guide us — through our spirits.*

Many times, however, we seek guidance by means other than the way God said. When we do, we get into trouble. We sometimes judge how God is leading by what our physical senses tell us. But nowhere does God say that God will guide us through our physical senses. Too often we look at things from a mental standpoint and endeavor to reason out things. But nowhere does the Bible say God will guide us through our mentality. The Bible does not say that the body of man is the candle of the Lord, nor that the mind of man is the candle of the Lord. It says that the spirit of man is the candle of the Lord.

God will guide us — He will enlighten us — through our spirits.

Now before we can understand how God does lead us

and guide us through our spirits, we have to understand the nature of man. We have to understand that man is a spirit, that he has a soul, and that he lives in a body.

Chapter 2
Man: An Eternal Spirit

And God said, Let us make man in our image,
after our likeness: . . . So God created man in his
own image, in the image of God created he him.
— Genesis 1:26,27

Man is a spirit being. He is made in the likeness of God. Jesus said that God is a Spirit (John 4:24). So man must of necessity be a spirit.

Man is a spirit, he has a soul, and he lives in a physical body (1 Thess. 5:23).

When the physical body of man is dead and in the grave, the spirit lives on. That part of man is eternal. Spirits can never die, and man is a spirit. Paul is speaking of physical death here:

PHILIPPIANS 1:23,24
23 For I am in a strait betwixt two, having a desire to depart, and to be with Christ; which is far better:
24 Nevertheless to abide in the flesh is more needful for you.

Paul is going to live. Whether in the body or out of the body, he is still going to live. If he abides, or lives in the flesh he can teach the church at Philippi and be a blessing to them. That would be more needful for them. It would be far better for Paul himself, however, to depart and be with Christ. Paul was actually saying, "I am going to live in the body or I am going to depart and be with Christ."

Who is going to depart?

"*I*" am going to depart. Paul was not talking about his body. His body was not going to depart. Paul is talking about the inward man, the spirit man, who lives inside the body.

3

People sometimes ask, "Will we know one another in Heaven?"

I always quickly ask, "Do you know one another down here?"

You see, *you* are the one who is going to be there. If *you* know one another down here, *you* will know one another there. *You* are the one who is here, and *you* will be the one who is there.

"*I* am going to depart," Paul says, "and be with Christ which is *far better.*" I like that! If he had just said it was better, that would have been good. But he said, "It is *far better!*"

Some false cults teach that when a man dies he is dead like a dog is dead when it dies. No, man is not. Man is more than a body. He is a spirit, he has a soul, and he lives in a body. Others say that when man dies he is in "soul sleep." The Bible does not teach that. Some say the spirit does depart all right — but it comes back as a cow, a dog, or as someone else. Reincarnation is unscriptural and unbiblical. Stay with the Word of God and it will solve all your problems along this line. Paul said, "*I* am going to depart. *I* am going to be with the Lord, which is *far better.*"

Paul preached the same truths and taught the same facts to all the churches. Here he uses different words to teach the same blessed truth to the church at Corinth:

2 CORINTHIANS 4:16
16 . . .but though our outward man perish, yet the inward man is renewed day by day.

There is an *inward* man. And there is an *outward* man. The outward man is not the real you. The outward man is only the house in which you live. The inward man is the real you. The inward man never grows older. He is renewed day by day. The inward man is a spirit man.

What is our spirit? Keep in mind our introductory texts. Romans 8:14 says, *". . . as many as are led by the Spirit of God, they are the sons of God."* Then verse 16 gives us a little insight into how the Spirit of God leads us: *"The Spirit itself* [Himself] *beareth witness with our spirit, that we are the children of God."* In other words, the Spirit of God bears witness with the spirit of man. Proverbs 20:27 says, *"The spirit of man is the candle of the Lord. . . ."* According to these scriptures God will guide us through our spirits; therefore, we must find out what our spirit is.

Jesus said to Nicodemus, *". . . Except a man be born again, he cannot see the kingdom of God"* (John 3:3).

Nicodemus, being natural, could only think naturally. So he said, *". . . How can a man be born when he is old? can he enter the second time into his mother's womb, and be born?"* (v. 4).

Jesus was not talking about a physical birth. He said, *"That which is born of the flesh is flesh; and that which is born of the Spirit is spirit"* (v. 6). He was talking about a *spiritual* birth.

The part of man that is born again is his spirit. Man's spirit receives *eternal life* — the life of God, and the nature of God. It is man's spirit that is made a new creature in Christ.

Paul calls man's spirit "the inward man." Peter calls man's spirit "the hidden man of the heart."

1 PETER 3:4
4 But let it be the hidden man of the heart, in that which is not corruptible, even the ornament of a meek and quiet spirit, which is in the sight of God of great price.

In many places when the Bible speaks of the heart, it is speaking of the spirit. This is the real man. It will help you in your believing and in your faith to think like that.

In the New Testament, wherever the word *heart* is used, substitute the word *spirit* and you will get a clearer picture of what the Bible is talking about. It is the spirit of man that is born again.

2 CORINTHIANS 5:17
17 Therefore if any man be in Christ, he is a new creature: old things are passed away; behold, all things are become new.

This is talking about the inward man. It couldn't be talking about the outward man. When you are born again and become a new creature, you do not get a new body. The outward man is just like it was before. If you were bald before you were born again, you are still bald afterwards. If you had brown eyes before, you still have brown eyes. The outward man does not change. God does not do anything with the outward man. (You have to do something with the outward man. You find out what God wants you to do with the outward man from the Bible — and then *you* do it.) God does something with the inward man. He makes the man on the inside a new man in Christ, a new creature — a new creation.

Chapter 3
Spirit-Conscious

*. . . I pray God your whole spirit and soul and
body be preserved blameless. . . .*
— 1 Thessalonians 5:23

In this scriptural passage, Paul begins with the inside,
the innermost part of man, the heart of his being, which
is his spirit, and comes to the outside.

Yet most people misquote this verse. They say, body,
soul, and spirit. Why do they put the body first? Because
they are more body-conscious than spirit-conscious.
Natural things mean more to them than spiritual things.
So they put physical things first.

Sometimes we are more mental-conscious because we
live more in the mental realm.

But man is a spirit being. We need to be spirit-
conscious. Spiritual things will become more real to us the
more spirit-conscious we become.

If we are going to be led by the Spirit of God, we must
become more spirit-conscious, or we'll miss out on the
whole thing. God's Spirit leads us through our spirits.

Put spirit first. Become more spirit-conscious, more
conscious of the inward man. Realize that you are a spirit
being and that you became a new creation created by God
in Christ Jesus. It will help you grow — *spiritually.*

Many years ago I began to think like this, and at first
I would say it to myself out loud: *I am a spirit being. I
have a soul. And I live in a body.*

Saying that helped me become more spirit-conscious.
It helped my faith, because faith is of the spirit, or the
heart.

Chapter 4
What Is the Difference
Between Spirit and Soul?

For the word of God is quick, and powerful, and sharper than any two-edged sword, piercing even to the dividing asunder of soul and spirit.... — Hebrews 4:12

The spirit and the soul are not the same.

Many years ago, back in the early 50's, I began an intensive study on this subject. I got books from the leading Bible schools and seminaries, both Pentecostal and denominational, to see what they taught on the subject of man. None satisfied me. None were actually scriptural. They were only scriptural, as the Bible says, "in part." I asked leading Bible scholars and ministers across the nation. You would recognize some of their names if I mentioned them. I even heard someone ask one of today's most well-known ministers, "What is the difference between the spirit and the soul?" He looked startled and said, "I thought they were the same." That was the answer I got from most of the ministers I asked.

Yet how could they be the same? Paul, by the Spirit of God, said they can be divided by the Word of God (Heb. 4:12). If you can divide them, they cannot be the same.

Only the Word of God can divide the spirit and the soul, however. The reason we have not been able to distinguish between them is that we have not dug deeply enough into the Word. Years ago, in the western part of the United States, they had what we call "the gold rush." People rushed out West. They were going to get rich in a hurry. Most panned a little gold out of creeks. Some found a few nuggets lying on the ground. But if you really wanted to strike it rich, you had to dig for it. The same is true in spiritual matters: You can skim along on the surface of the Bible and pan out a little gold here and there — and even find a nugget occasionally. But if you really want to strike it rich, you have to dig down deep into the Word of God.

For 15 years I studied carefully, burning the midnight oil. If there was anything I desired to know it was the difference between the spirit and the soul. Eventually, I went through this process of elimination. I wrote it down like this: *With my body I contact the physical realm.* (That goes without argument.) *With my spirit I contact the spiritual realm.* That left only one other part of me that made contact with any other realm. I knew then that it had to be with my soul that I contacted the intellectual or soulish realm (which includes the emotions and the intellect). So I wrote: *With my soul I contact the intellectual realm.* Here is a scripture that helped me:

> **1 CORINTHIANS 14:14**
> **14 For if I pray in an unknown tongue, my spirit prayeth, but my understanding is unfruitful.**

The Amplified translation reads, "For if I pray in an [unknown] tongue, my spirit [by the Holy Spirit within me] prays, but my mind is unproductive. . . ."

Our understanding, our natural human mentality, is a part of our soul.

Notice what Paul said. "My spirit prays, but my understanding is unfruitful." He did not say, "When I pray in an unknown tongue my soul prays." He did not say, "When I pray in tongues, I pray out of my intellect, or out of my mind." He said in effect, "I am not praying out of my soul when I pray in tongues; I am praying out of my spirit, my heart, my innermost being." Do you remember what Jesus said?

JOHN 7:37-39
37 In the last day, that great day of the feast, Jesus stood and cried, saying, If any man thirst, let him come unto me, and drink.
38 He that believeth on me, as the scripture hath said, OUT OF HIS BELLY shall flow rivers of living water.
39 (BUT THIS SPAKE HE OF THE SPIRIT, which they that believe on him should receive: for the Holy Ghost was not yet given; because that Jesus was not yet glorified.)

As a result of receiving the Holy Spirit, Jesus said, "out of the belly shall flow rivers of living water." Another translation reads, "out of the innermost being will flow rivers of living water."

A Full Gospel pastor's daughter was six years old when she and some of the children were off by themselves one night at a revival. Some of these youngsters were filled with the Holy Spirit and began to speak with other tongues. This little six-year-old, holding her stomach, ran up to her mother, saying, "Momma, Momma, that came right out of my belly."

She was being scriptural. She was speaking in tongues from her belly — her spirit, her innermost being. That's where tongues come from — the Holy Spirit who resides in your spirit gives your spirit the utterance and you speak it out.

Consider these scriptures together now. *"The spirit of man is the candle of the Lord, searching all the INWARD PARTS OF THE BELLY ... OUT OF HIS BELLY shall flow rivers of living water...."*

All the leadings I have ever received have come from out of my spirit. And most of them have come while I was praying in other tongues. You can understand why. Your spirit is active when you are praying in tongues.

One reason the church world as a whole has failed so miserably is that it has done so much of just one kind of praying — praying with the understanding, or *mental* praying. Christians have endeavored to fight spiritual battles with mental abilities.

I have learned this through these many, many years. In every crisis of life I have learned to look to my spirit inside me. I have learned to pray in other tongues. While I am praying in other tongues, guidance comes up from inside me. This is because my spirit is active. My body is not active, my mind (my soul) is not active, but my spirit is active, and it is through my spirit that God is going to guide me.

Sometimes I interpret what I am praying in tongues, and through the interpretation I receive light and guidance (1 Cor. 14:13). But most of the time, that is not so. Most of the time, just while I am praying in tongues, from somewhere way down inside, I can sense something rise up in me. It begins to take shape and form. I cannot tell anyone mentally how I know it, because my understanding has nothing to do with it. But I know on the inside of me what to do.

I follow that. I listen to my spirit. Because the spirit of man is the candle of the Lord.

Chapter 5
The Saving of the Soul

... receive with meekness the engrafted word, which is able to save your souls.
— James 1:21

The spirit of man is the part of man that is born again. It is the part of man that receives *eternal life,* which is the nature and life of God. It is the spirit of man that becomes a new creature in Christ Jesus. The soul is not the innermost being at all. It is not the soul that is born again. The saving of the soul is a process.

James 1:21 used to bother me when I was a denominational preacher before I was filled with the Holy Spirit. I didn't know what I know now. I used spirit and soul interchangeably — referring to the spirit as the soul, and the soul as the spirit. I didn't divide them as the Bible does. But I did have enough sense to leave this verse alone until I grew so that I could understand what it is saying.

The Epistle of James was not written to sinners. James did not write a letter to the world; he wrote this letter to the Church. We know that because of James 5 where he says, *"Is any sick among you? let him call for the elders of the church ..."* (v. 14). In other words, if there is any sick among the Church, let him call for the elders of the Church. Also referring back now to the first chapter of James, let's pick up with verse 18:

JAMES 1:18-21
18 Of his own will begat he us with the word of truth, that we should be a kind of firstfruits of his creatures.
19 Wherefore, my beloved brethren, let every man be swift to hear, slow to speak, slow to wrath:
20 For the wrath of man worketh not the righteousness of God.
21 Wherefore lay apart all filthiness and superfluity of

naughtiness, and receive with meekness the engrafted
word, which is able to save your souls.

James is talking to born-again believers. Of the
Father's own will, he writes, we were begotten, or born
again by the Word of Truth. He calls them "my beloved
brethren," so they were in Christ. Yet he encourages these
born-again, Spirit-filled people to receive the engrafted
Word with meekness, "... *which is able to save your
souls.*" Evidently, their souls were not saved.

You see, a man's spirit, the innermost man, the real
man, receives eternal life and is born again. But his
intellect and emotions — which comprise his soul — still
have to be dealt with. They are not born again. They are
to be renewed.

Paul speaks about the renewing of the mind, writing
to the saints at Rome.

ROMANS 12:2
2 And be not conformed to this world: but be ye
transformed by the renewing of your mind, that ye may
prove what is that good, and acceptable, and perfect, will
of God.

The Psalmist David spoke of the restoring of the soul:

PSALM 23:3
3 He restoreth my soul ...

The Hebrew word translated *restore* in the Old Testament, and the Greek word translated *renew* in the New
Testament mean about the same thing. The soul — the
mind — is to be renewed or restored.

My mother left me a chair which she inherited from
her mother. I don't know exactly how old that chair is,
but it is quite old. I can remember when my grandmother
had it restored. They put new upholstery on it. They revar-

nished it. It was still the same chair; it was just restored.
It was renewed.

In the Word it is never written that God restores our
spirits. Our spirits become brand-new creatures in Christ
Jesus. Our souls, however, must be renewed or restored.

How? We have these scriptures relative to the soul:
*receive with meekness the engrafted word, which is able
to save your souls . . . be not conformed to this world: but
be ye transformed by the renewing of your mind, that ye
may prove what is that good, and acceptable, and perfect,
will of God . . . He restoreth my soul* (James 1:21;
Rom. 12:2; Ps. 23:3).

Man's soul is saved, or restored, when his mind
becomes renewed with the Word of God. It is the Word
of God that saves our souls, that renews our minds, that
restores our souls.

When our minds become renewed with the Word of
God, then we think in line with what God's Word says.
We are able to know and prove the permissive and the
perfect will of God — because the Word of God is the will
of God. We don't have so many questions about the will
of God once we get our souls saved.

The greatest need in the Church today is to have minds
renewed with the Word of God.

Chapter 6
Presenting the Body

> *I beseech you therefore, brethren, by the mercies of God, that ye present your bodies a living sacrifice, holy, acceptable unto God, which is your reasonable service.* — Romans 12:1

It is the inward man — not the outward man — that becomes a new creature in Christ. We still have the same body we had before we became a new creature. What we must learn to do is to let that new man on the inside of us dominate. With that new man, we control the flesh and do something with our bodies.

Let's look again at Second Corinthians 5:17 which says, *"Therefore if any man be in Christ, he is a new creature: old things are passed away; behold, all things are become new."* One translation reads, "If any man be in Christ, there is a new self. . . ."

Sometimes in churches we hear people talk about "dying out to self." There is no such statement in the Bible. We don't need to die out to self if we have become a new self. What we need to do is crucify the flesh. The Bible does talk about that.

Crucifying the flesh is not something God does for you. It is something you do for yourself. *"I beseech you therefore, brethren,"* Paul wrote to the Church, *"by the mercies of God, that ye present your bodies ..."* (Rom. 12:1).

Who presents your body?

You do.

Who is you?

That's the man on the inside who is born again, and has become a new creature.

You do something with your body. If *you* do not do

something with it, nothing will ever be done with it.

1 CORINTHIANS 9:27
27 But I keep under my body, and bring it into subjection:
lest that by any means, when I have preached to others,
I myself should be a castaway [disapproved].

Here Paul is talking about the fact that *he* does
something with his body. "*I* keep under my body. *I* bring
it into subjection."

Who is *I*?

That's the real man — the real Paul — the man on the
inside who has become a new creature in Christ Jesus and
is filled with the Holy Spirit. "*I* do something with my
body. *I* keep it under. *I* bring it into subjection."

What did Paul bring his body into subjection to?

To the inward man. Instead of letting the body
dominate the inward man, Paul saw to it that the inward
man dominated the outward man.

Now notice this. Here is this great apostle, this holy
man of God, this man who wrote half the New Testament,
a man who is a spiritual giant — yet evidently his body
wanted to do things that were wrong. If it hadn't, he would
not have had to keep it under. He would not have had to
bring it into subjection.

Just because your body wants to do wrong, doesn't
mean you are not saved, or that you are not filled with
the Holy Spirit. (If that were the case, Paul was not saved.)
You will have to contend with the body, the flesh, as long
as you are in this world.

"Brother Hagin, I want you to pray for me," one man
said.

"What for?" I asked. I like to know what I am praying for.

A look of seriousness, even tears, came to his eyes, "I
want you to pray that I will never have any more trouble

with the devil.''

I said, "Do you want me to pray you will die?"

"No, no, I don't want to die."

I said, "The only way you won't have any more trouble with the devil is to get out of here and go on to Heaven."

You will have problems with the devil as long as you are in this life. You will have problems with the flesh as long as you are in the flesh. But, blessed be God, the means, the ability, and the authority have been given to you through the Word of God to deal with the devil and to deal with the flesh.

Paul did not let his body dominate him. The man on the inside that was born again and filled with the Holy Spirit — must dominate the outward man.

You can do it. What I want you to see is this — *you* are the one who *must* do it. Paul did not say God would do it for you. He did not say the Holy Spirit would do it for you. He said, "*You* present your bodies." He said, "*You* be not conformed to this world." He said, "*You* be transformed by the renewing of your mind." *You* present your body. *You* do it. *You* get your mind renewed with the Word of God. *You* do it.

The life and nature of God is inside your spirit. Let that man on the inside be the dominant one. Listen to him. It is the spirit of man that is the candle of the Lord. It is through your spirit that God will guide you.

Chapter 7
Number One:
The Inward Witness

The Spirit itself [Himself] *beareth witness with our spirit....*   — Romans 8:16

You will find that being led by the inward witness is the number one way, or the primary way, that God leads all of His children.

Let me go back — I said I would in the preface of this book — to what Jesus said to me in February 1959 in El Paso, Texas. It was 6:30 in the evening. I was sitting up in bed studying. My eyes were wide open. (There are three types of visions. The highest type is an open vision. In an open vision, one's physical senses are not suspended, and his physical eyes are not closed. He possesses all of his physical capabilities, yet sees into the realm of the spirit.)

I heard footsteps. The door to my room was ajar twelve to fourteen inches, so I looked to see who was coming into my room. I expected to see some literal, physical person. But as I looked to see who it was, I saw Jesus. It seemed as if the hair on my neck and head stood straight up on end. Chill bumps popped out all over my body.

I saw Him. He had on a white robe. He wore Roman sandals. (Jesus has appeared to me eight times. Every time, except this time, His feet were bare. This time He had on sandals; that's what I had heard as He approached my door.) He seemed to be about 5 feet 11 inches tall. He looked as if He weighed about 180 pounds.

He came through the door and pushed it back until it was almost shut. He walked around the foot of my bed. I followed Him with my eyes — almost spellbound. He took ahold of a straight chair and pushed it up close to my bed. Then He sat down on it, folded His hands, and began His conversation with me by saying, "I told you in the automobile the other night. . . ."

The automobile had been full. My wife and I and others were driving along within two blocks of where I now was, as Jesus sat by my bedside talking to me. In the car, I had heard the Spirit of God speak to me. I thought everyone in the car had heard it and I said, "Did you all hear that?" They said, "No, we didn't hear anything."

In the Old Testament the prophets would say, "And the Word of the Lord came unto me saying. . . ." Did you ever wonder how it came? It could not have been literally audible. If it had been audible everyone present would have heard it — the prophet would not have had to tell the people what the Spirit said. The Word of the Lord came to the prophet's spirit from the Spirit of God. It is so real that it seems audible at the time. The Word of the Lord was so real to me, I thought everyone in the car with me had heard it too.

As Jesus sat at my bedside, He said, "I spoke to you the night before last in the automobile and told you certain things. I told you, by my Spirit, that later I would talk to you further. So now I have come to talk to you about this. . . ."

It was concerning the ministry of the prophet. Jesus sat there in that chair and talked to me for an hour and a half. And I talked to Him. I asked questions in reference to what He was saying. He answered them. I will not go into all He said about the prophet's ministry; that is another message. But I will get into some of it.

Jesus said to me, "The prophet of the New Testament is very similar to the prophet of the Old Testament in that the prophet of the Old Testament was called a 'seer' because he saw and knew things supernaturally. The prophet of the New Testament also sees and knows things supernaturally. But the prophet of the New Testament does not have the same status as the prophet of the Old Testament, in that I did not set prophets in the Church to guide the Church. A Christian under the New Testament need not seek guidance through prophets. He might receive guidance through prophets, but he should not seek it. It is unscriptural to do so. The ministry of the New Testament prophet in this area is only to confirm what people already have in their own spirits.

"Under the Old Covenant, only the priest, the prophet, and the king were anointed by the Holy Spirit to stand in those offices. What you would call the laity did not have the Spirit of God upon them or in them. Therefore, under the Old Covenant, people would seek guidance through the prophet because he had the Spirit of God."

Under the New Testament, thanks be to God, we not only have the Spirit of God *upon* us — we have Him *in* us!

Jesus also said to me, "Under the New Covenant, it does not say, 'As many as are led by prophets, they are the sons of God.' The New Testament says, *'For as many as are led by the Spirit of God, they are the sons of God'* " (Rom. 8:14).

Then He said, "The number one way, the primary way, that I lead all of My children is by the inward witness. I am going to show you how that works so you won't make the mistakes you have made in the past."

Jesus explained to me that to stand in the office of the prophet, one is first of all a minister of the gospel separated and called to the ministry with the call of God upon his life. Secondly, he has at least two of the revelation gifts — the word of wisdom, the word of knowledge, the discerning of spirits — plus the gift of prophecy, operating in his ministry.

Then He called my attention to something that had been happening to me for the previous three days. For the past three days, I had sat down to write a letter to a pastor confirming a date to hold a meeting for him. Somehow, the first day, I got about half a page written, then I tore it up and threw it into the wastebasket. The next day I did the same thing. The third day I did the same thing. Then it was the day that the Lord was here in the room talking to me.

Jesus said, "You see Me sitting here talking to you. This is a manifestation of the Spirit called discerning of spirits. (Discerning of spirits is seeing into the spirit realm.) This is the prophet's ministry in operation. You are seeing into the realm of the spirit. You see Me. You hear Me talking. I am bringing you, through the vision, a word of knowledge and also a word of wisdom. I am telling you not to go to that church. The pastor would not accept the way you would minister when you got there. But I am never going to lead you this way again. (He never has, and that was many years ago.) From now on, I'm going to lead you by the inward witness. You had the inward witness all the time. You had a *check* in your spirit. That's the reason you tore up the letter three times. You had *something* on the inside, a *check,* a *red light,* a *stop signal.* It wasn't even a voice that said, 'Don't go.' It was just an *inward intuition.*"

Then Jesus reminded me of another invitation. I had preached a convention for one of the Full Gospel denominations the previous year. Nearly every pastor there asked me if I would come and hold a meeting. I had hundreds of calls, I suppose.

One fellow came up to me and said, "Brother Hagin, do you ever go to small churches?"

I said, "I go anywhere the Lord says to go."

"Well, we only run seventy to ninety in Sunday School. But if God ever speaks to you, we want you to come."

I dismissed that conversation along with many others.

Several months later, however, while praying in the church one day about my services that night, that conversation came back to me. Then every day it continued to come back to me. Finally, after about thirty or forty days, I said, "Lord, do You want me to go to that little church for a meeting?"

The more I would pray about it and the more I would think about it, as we say, the better I would feel about it on the inside of me. It wasn't a physical feeling, but it was a feeling in my spirit.

Sitting by my bedside, Jesus referred to this: "The more you thought about it, the better you felt about it. You had a *velvety-like* feeling in your spirit. That's the *green light.* That's the *go-ahead signal.* That's the *witness of the Spirit* to go. Now you see Me sitting here, you hear Me talking to you, and I am telling you to go to that church. But I am never going to lead you to go anywhere like this again. (He never has.) From now on, I am going to lead you just like I do every other Christian — by the inward witness."

Then the Lord said this to me, which is not just for my benefit, but also for yours: "If you will learn to follow that inward witness, I will make you rich. I will guide you in all the affairs of life, financial as well as spiritual. [Some think God is only interested in their spiritual well-being, and nothing else. But He is interested in everything we are interested in.] I am not opposed to My children being rich; I am opposed to their being covetous."

I have followed that inward witness and He has done just what He said He would do. He has made me rich.

Someone asked, "Are you a millionaire?"

I didn't say that. Some people fail to realize what the word "rich" means. It means *a full supply.* It means *abundant provision.* I have more than a full supply. I have more than an abundant provision. It is because I learned to follow the leading of the Spirit by the inward witness.

What He did for me, He will do for you. It won't come overnight, or by next Saturday night. But as you learn to develop your spirit and follow that inward witness, He will guide you in every area of your life.

I knew a man down in Texas. He had never worn a pair of shoes until he was 12 years old. He only had a fifth grade education. But way back when money was money, he was a millionaire.

Two different people, one from California and the other from Minnesota who had been frequent house guests in his home, told me that this man told each of them the same thing.

He said to them both, "In all these years and in all these investments [that's how he made his money], I have never lost a dime."

That beats my record. How about yours?

"Everything I have ever invested in, has made money," he told each of them on different occasions. Then he told them how he did it.

"I always do this. When someone comes along with an idea, wanting me to invest in something, my first reaction is mental. Now I know when Jesus said, 'When you pray, enter into your closet,' that He didn't necessarily mean you have to get into a closet to pray. I know He meant for us to shut things out. But I have a large closet in my bedroom where I go to pray. I pray about it. I wait long enough — until I hear what my spirit says. Sometimes I wait three days. Now I don't mean that I stay in there 24 hours a day. I might come out and eat one meal. Usually I miss a few. I come out and sleep a little bit. But the majority of the time I am waiting, just by myself, until I know inside by an inward witness what I am to do.

"Sometimes my head says, 'Boy, you would be a fool to put your money in that. You'll lose your shirt.' But my heart says, 'Go ahead and invest in it.' So I do. And in all these years, I have never lost a dime.

"Then again, someone comes along with a deal and my head says, 'Boy, you had better get in on that one.' But I don't pay any attention to my head. I get in that closet and wait. Sometimes all night long I wait. I'll pray and read my Bible, but a lot of the time I just wait. I just get quiet until I can hear inside what my heart says. When my heart says, 'No, don't do it,' and my head says, 'Yes, you'd better get in on it,' I don't do it."

What had this man done? He had learned to follow the inward witness and God had guided him in his business, until in the late 1930's and the early 1940's he was already worth two million dollars. That doesn't sound big now, but it was big then.

Do you think God loved him more than He loves you? No, but this man took time to listen to God. *He took steps and means and measures to wait upon God.*

I was with a group of ministers and we were talking personally, and conversing with one another. Someone asked a certain individual who is a very successful minister, "Now we know that God called you and that the anointing of God's Spirit is upon you. But from your standpoint, is there any one thing you do that you would say has contributed more to your success than any other *one* thing?"

That man said, "I always follow my deepest premonitions."

What was he saying? He was simply saying, "I always listen to my spirit. I do what my spirit tells me to do. I follow that inward witness."

The inward witness is just as supernatural as guidance through visions and so on; it is just not as spectacular. Many people are looking for the spectacular and missing the supernatural that is right there all the time.

Chapter 8
Know-So Salvation

He that believeth on the Son of God hath the
witness in himself....   — 1 John 5:10

For as many as are led by the Spirit of God, they are
the sons of God" (Rom. 8:14). The sons of God can expect
to be led by the Spirit of God. Hallelujah! They are not
led by someone else telling them what to do. The Holy
Spirit is going to lead us. We have Scripture that says so.

How does He lead? Verse 16 gives us a clue: *"The Spirit*
itself [Himself] *BEARETH WITNESS with our spirit,*
that we are the children of God" (Rom. 8:16).

In the most important aspect of life, and in the most
important thing that can happen to you — becoming a
child of God — God lets you know that you are His child
by His Spirit *bearing witness* with your spirit. Then you
can understand that the first and foremost way God will
lead you is also by that inward witness.

You do not know that you are a child of God because
someone prophesied that you are. You wouldn't accept
that. You do not know that you are a child of God because
someone said, "I *feel* like you are." You wouldn't accept
that. You are not a child of God because you had a vision.
You might, or you might not have had a vision, but a vision
is not what would make you a child of God. That is not
what the Bible says. That is not the way you know you
are a child of God.

How does the Bible say we know we are children of
God? *His Spirit, God's Spirit, bears witness with our*
spirits.

Sometimes you can't really explain how you know you
are a child of God, but you just know it, right down on
the inside of you. You know it! You know you are by the

inward witness.

I was born again as a teenager on the bed of sickness April 22, 1933. Since that day, the thought has never occurred to me that I might not be saved. Yet even as a young Christian I ran into people who said, "You're not saved because you don't belong to *our* church." Or those who would argue, "You're not saved because you haven't been baptized *our* way." And many gave me other reasons why they thought I was not saved.

But none of that disturbed me. I laughed at it, *because I had the witness! And I had the love!*

1 JOHN 3:14
14 We know that we have passed from death unto life, because we love....

Chapter 9
Fleeced!

A new heart also will I give you, and a new spirit will I put within you: and I will take away the stony heart out of your flesh, and I will give you an heart of flesh. And I will put my spirit within you. . . . — Ezekiel 36:26,27

In 1941 I didn't know as much as I know now. Please don't misunderstand me; I don't know as much now as I *am going* to know. I would hate to think I know all I am ever going to know in this life about God and about the Bible. No, we don't know everything, but praise God for what we do know.

Anyway, in 1941 My wife and I were pastors of a church in the blackland of North Central Texas. Another church down in the oil field of East Texas wanted me to come and try out as pastor. So I drove down and preached one Sunday. The church asked if they could vote on me for pastor, and I said yes. Traveling back home after the service, I put out a fleece.

Now I was born and raised Southern Baptist. I started preaching as a Southern Baptist. In 1937 I was baptized in the Holy Spirit as a Baptist preacher. In 1939 I accepted the pastorate of a little Full Gospel Church. It was in March 1941 that this church in East Texas wanted to consider me as pastor. I had been with Full Gospel people long enough by that time that some of their misconceptions had rubbed off on me. Don't misunderstand me; a lot of good things rubbed off on me too. But this one was bad. I kept hearing them talk about putting out fleeces. So I put out a fleece.

I really knew better. But at the time it seemed as if it would save me a lot of the trouble of praying, and getting alone and waiting on God, and maybe some fasting — just to put out a fleece.

In putting out a fleece, one prays something like this: "Lord, if you want me to do this — then You do that." Or, "God, if you want me to do this, then have that happen." Or, "Lord, shut that door, and open this door."

Some of those doors the devil might shut, and some of them the devil might open. They are in his territory. The Bible calls him the god of this world (2 Cor. 4:4). That would be like praying, "Lord, if you want me to go to Kansas City next week, You open Brother Hagin's front door." I might open it myself. I live there. You see, Satan can move in the sense realm.

God has a better way of leading His children than by a hit-and-miss method such as fleeces. The New Testament does not say, "As many as are led by fleeces, they are the children of God."

"Yes," someone might say, "but Gideon put out a fleece back in the Old Testament."

Why go back under the Old Covenant? We have something better. The Old Covenant is for spiritually dead people. I am not spiritually dead. I am alive! I have the Spirit of God in me.

Remember Gideon was not a prophet, a priest, or a king. Only those three offices, under the Old Covenant, were anointed by the Spirit of God. The Spirit of God was not personally present with the rest of the people.

That's why every male had to present himself at the temple in Jerusalem once a year. The Shekinah glory — the Presence of God — was kept shut up in the Holy of Holies. But when Jesus died on Calvary, the curtain that curtained off the Holy of Holies was rent (torn) in twain from top to bottom — and God moved out. He has never dwelled in earth-made houses since. He dwells in us!

It is dangerous for New Testament, Spirit-filled Chris-

tians to put out fleeces. I know that from the Word. And
I know it from experience.

Back there in 1941 I said as I drove along, "Lord, I
am going to put out a fleece. I am just going to turn it
over to You. (I didn't realize that I wasn't turning it over
to the Lord.) If they elect me as pastor one hundred percent, I am going to accept that as being the will of God,
and I am going to accept that church."

I got every vote! That was my fleece. They elected me
100 percent. They missed God. I missed God. They got
fleeced. I got fleeced. I got out of the perfect will of God —
and God just let me do it.

We moved into the parsonage. Many things were more
comfortable than what we'd had before, from the natural
standpoint. We had more money. We lived in a better parsonage. We drove a better automobile.

But I would study and pray and get a message — and
be just all on fire. Then the minute I stepped inside the
church door, it was as though somebody poured a bucket
of cold water on me. I lost it all. In fourteen months I
didn't preach a decent sermon. No inspiration.

My wife was reluctant to say anything. She finally did
say, "Honey, you've got to where you can make a pretty
good talk."

That was all I was doing, making "talks." I wasn't
preaching. When my agreed-upon time was up, I left. I
didn't wait for some signal to leave; I just left.

Later on in pastoring, I always wanted to go back there
for a meeting because I wanted those people to know I
could preach. They had never really heard me *preach*.
Finally, in the course of time, I went back and held a
revival. Folks' mouths fell open. "We didn't know you
could preach like that," they said.

I said, "Oh, yes, I preached like that before I came here
to pastor, and I preached like that after I left here."

"Well, you didn't preach like that when you were here."

I said, "No, because we were all out of the will of God. I was here out of the will of God, and you elected me out of the will of God."

I learned about that fleece business. One time ought to cure a fellow. But some folks — even though none of their fleeces have ever worked — still put out fleeces.

I never missed it again in going to any other church as pastor. And I didn't put out any more fleeces. I prayed and waited on God. I talked to God long enough so that I knew right on the inside what I was to do.

Chapter 10
Following the Witness

*For thou wilt light my candle: the Lord my
God will enlighten my darkness.*— Psalm 18:28

We left that church. We were asked by leaders of a
denomination to take another church to fill in temporarily,
so we did.

Later, while I would be in my study praying, I would
get a burden to go back to the church I'd left as a result
of the fleece. I hadn't finished what God wanted me to do
there.

Usually this happened when I was praying about my
sermon and the Sunday services in other tongues —
because remember, when I pray in tongues, my spirit
prays, and the spirit of man is the candle of the Lord. I
would get such a burden for the church I had left more
than two years before, I would jump up and run out of
the room to get away from it.

Once I came to myself out in the street beside the
church wondering, *How did I get out here?* To get out there
I would have had to run out of the church study, across
the auditorium, and out the side door. But I didn't
remember doing that. I was under such a burden for that
church, and I was trying to get away from it. I didn't want
to go back there to pastor.

Finally, after about 30 days of that, I said, "Lord, are
You talking to me about going back there? Are You trying to give me some guidance?" Then I said, "Talk to my
wife. She can listen too."

One morning while we washed dishes, I said to my wife,
"Honey, if the Lord says anything to you, let me know."
I didn't tell her anything more.

Then I waited 30 days. You don't have to get in a big

hurry about some things. The Bible says, "*. . . he that believeth shall not make haste*" (Isa. 28:16). Faith doesn't get in a hurry. The devil will try to push you. He will say, "Hurry up. Hurry up. Hurry, hurry, hurry." He will try to move you out of faith, move you into doubt, move you into unbelief, and get you away from the leading of God.

Thirty days later, as I washed the dishes and my wife dried them, I said, "Has the Lord been talking to you?"

"If He has, I don't know it."

I got a little more pointed in order to bring her out. I said, "Has the Lord said anything to you about going back to _____?" I called the name of the city where the church was.

"Oh," she said, "I thought that was just me."

"Well," I said, "let's analyze what you mean when you say *me*."

If you mean the flesh, then that wouldn't be right. But if you mean the real "me," the man on the inside — the real *you* — then that is right. Remember that the spirit is the candle of the Lord. Then it is not just you, the outward man, *it is the Lord lighting the candle for you* — the inward man — the man on the inside.

"I want to ask you a question," I said to her, "so we can ascertain just which this is. From the physical, from the mental, just naturally speaking, do you want to go back there?"

"Oh, no!"

"It couldn't be you then, could it? (It would have been better to say, it couldn't have been the flesh, the natural man, the outward man.) You're not going to be thinking about doing something you don't want to do."

I saw she had the inward witness just as I did. Sometimes the inward witness is there and people don't recognize it.

"I am convinced," I told her, "that God is leading us

that way. It will have to be God to open it up and get us back there. Let's just let Him do it."

He did. Within a few months, without my doing anything to work it out, I was invited to preach a week in that church. Afterwards, the board asked if I would be interested in coming back to pastor.

I didn't tell them I had something from God. I just said, "I might be."

They said, "We have all been talking and the church wants you back."

"Well," I said, "they would have to vote on me. So I'll tell you what I'll do — just go ahead and vote, and I will tell you afterwards."

From the natural standpoint my wife and I still did not want to go back there. Although we loved the people, we did not want to live in that town. We did not want to live in that house. In my heart I wanted to obey God, but everything about my flesh recoiled. In my natural man, my outward man, and in my own natural human thinking and mind, I did not want to go back there.

So really, as I kept praying and fasting while the church board was making all the proper announcements and advertising the election, I was actually saying to the Lord that I didn't want to trust that inward witness I knew both my wife and I had.

I was over into the third day of a fast. I wanted the Lord to move in some *spectacular* way — I wanted some kind of a word, tongues and interpretation, a prophecy, or God just to write up in the sky, "GO TO THAT PLACE." I was on my knees bawling and squawling and begging — because I didn't know any better.

God also leads by an inward voice as well as by an inward witness. That inward voice said, "Get up from there and quit acting like that."

I got up. Then I said, "Lord, if You could just give me

some supernatural sign, I would feel better about this.''

He said, "You have all I am going to give you. You don't need any supernatural sign. You don't need any supernatural writing in the sky. You don't need any tongues and interpretation. You don't need any prophecy. You know on the inside of you what to do. Now do it.''

I said, "Okay, I will.''

Many times we ignore the inward witness. We want something out in the sense realm. We seek the sensational and miss the supernatural.

Let's learn that God leads all of His children, *primarily,* by the inward witness.

Chapter 11
Number Two:
The Inward Voice

*I say the truth in Christ, I lie not, my con-
science also bearing me witness in the Holy
Ghost.*   — Romans 9:1

The number one way the Spirit guides us is through
the inward witness. Number two is by the inward voice.

The inward man, who is a spirit man, has a voice —
just as the outward man has a voice. We call this voice
of the inward man *conscience*. We call this voice the *still
small voice.*

Your spirit has a voice. Your spirit will speak to you.

In September 1966 we moved to Tulsa, Oklahoma, from
Garland, Texas, a suburb of Dallas. We had lived there
17 years. The move came about like this: My wife and I
were in Tulsa on business. The ministry was growing and
I had already figured out in my head what I would do with
my office and home in Texas to accommodate the growth.
But a friend with whom we were staying in Tulsa, said,
"Brother Hagin, you ought to move to Tulsa. Brother T. L.
Osborn's old office building is for sale. His business
manager asked me to sell it for them." Then he quoted
their price. It was extremely low. But I was not interested.
Finally, he said, "Let's go look at it." I went along just
to humor him.

The minute I stood inside that building a buzzer went
off inside of me. (Sometimes that inward witness is so real
it can almost sound like an inward "buzzer.") I knew as
well as I knew my name, *this is it!* But I didn't want to
listen to it; I wanted to stay in Garland.

(That's why we don't hear a lot of times. We don't want
to hear. We say we do, but we don't.)

Back at our friend's home, my wife asked me about the building.

"Oh, no. I've already got it all figured out. We'll stay where we are. We'll turn our whole home into an office. And we'll just stay in Garland."

We went to bed that night, but I couldn't sleep.

Ordinarily, I have no trouble sleeping. The Bible says, "*. . . he giveth his beloved sleep*" (Ps. 127:2). I am His beloved. So are you. "*. . . he hath made us accepted in the beloved*" (Eph. 1:6). So I always claim the promise of God and say, "Lord, I'm Your beloved. So I take You at Your Word. I thank You for sleep." And I always go to sleep.

But this time, I couldn't. My conscience was hurting. My conscience is the voice of my spirit. My spirit knows I didn't listen to it.

Lying there quietly in the nighttime, I said, "Lord, if you want me to move to Tulsa, I will. In the natural, I don't want to move there, but I wouldn't want to stand in Your way."

Then on the inside of me I heard the still small voice.

Now I'm not talking about the Spirit of God speaking. When the Holy Spirit speaks it is more authoritative. The still small voice is the voice of our own spirit speaking. But our own spirit picks it up from the Holy Spirit who is in us.

That still small voice, that inward voice, not authoritative, just something on the inside of me said, "I am going to give you that building."

I laughed. I know there is a lot of unbelief about this, but I said, "Okay. When you do, I'll believe it."

That inward voice, picking up on what the Holy Spirit was saying, said, "You watch me."

Without going into all the details, it would surprise you how God gave us that building.

Chapter 12
Effects of the Spirit's Indwelling

*And Paul, earnestly beholding the council,
said, Men and brethren, I have lived in all good
conscience before God until this day.*— Acts 23:1

It is interesting to go through the Epistles Paul wrote
to the Church and see what he said about his conscience.
You will notice that he always obeyed it.

Is your conscience a safe guide?

Yes, if your spirit has become a new man in Christ, it
is because your conscience is the voice of your spirit.

> 2 CORINTHIANS 5:17
> 17 Therefore if any man be in Christ, he is a new creature:
> old things are passed away; behold, all things are become
> new.

These things take place in man's spirit, in the inward
man. He is first a new creature — a brand-new man in
Christ. Second, old things have passed away — the nature
of the devil in his spirit is gone. Third, ALL things have
become new *in his spirit* — not in his body or in his mind —
now he has the nature of God in his spirit.

Therefore, if your spirit is a new man with the life and
nature of God in it, it is a safe guide.

A person who has not been born again could not follow
the voice of his spirit. His spirit is unregenerate. His conscience would permit him to do anything.

When you have the life and nature of God in you, your
conscience will not permit you to do just anything. And
if you are born again, you have the life of God.

> JOHN 3:16
> 16 For God so loved the world, that he gave his only

begotten Son, that whosoever believeth in him should not
perish, but have EVERLASTING LIFE.

ROMANS 6:23
23 For the wages of sin is death; but the gift of God is
ETERNAL LIFE through Jesus Christ our Lord.

Someone said, "That just means we are going to live
forever up in heaven."

No, it does not only mean that. Consider this scripture:

1 JOHN 5:13
13 These things have I written unto you that believe on
the name of the Son of God; that ye may know that YE
HAVE ETERNAL LIFE. . . .

Have is present tense. We have *eternal life* now. If you
are a born-again Christian, you have the *life of God* in your
spirit now. You have the *nature of God* in your spirit now.

Oh! If people would learn to follow their spirits! If they
would learn to take advantage of the life that is in them!

I joined the church and was baptized early in life —
but that didn't make me a Christian. My spirit was still
unregenerate when I became totally bedfast with a heart
condition at the age of 15. I was truly born again during
the 16 months I was bedfast. Then in August 1934, as a
Baptist boy reading Grandma's Methodist Bible, I was
healed.

I went back to high school. I had missed one school
year. Before I was born again, I just barely got by in some
classes. Back then, if you made a "D" it was failing. And
if you failed one subject you stayed in that grade and took
the whole thing over again. Two teachers in two subjects
said to me, "We gave you two points or you would have
had a 'D.' "

But after I was born again, I never made anything but
a straight "A" report card. And I never took one book

home to study.

Now I didn't know a thing about the baptism of the Holy Spirit then, but do you know what I did know? I knew I had the life of God in me!

As I walked down the street to school every morning, I had a conversation with the Lord. Unconsciously, I was being led by the Spirit; my heart told me to do it, and I listened to my heart instead of my head.

I said, "Now, Lord, I read in the Old Testament where Daniel and the three Hebrew children were in school in Babylon and You gave them favor with the dean of the school (Dan. 1:9). God, give me favor with every teacher. Thank You for it; I have it now. I also read, that when their three years of training were over, the three Hebrew children were ten times smarter than the rest (vv. 18-20). Lord, I have Your life in me. John 1:4 says, *'In him was life; and the life was the light of men.'* Light stands for development. Impart to me knowledge and skill in all learning and wisdom that I may be ten times better. . . ."

Every day as I walked to school I would confess, "In Him was life and the life was the light of men. That life is in me. The life of God is in me. That life is the light — it is the development of me. It is developing my spirit. It is developing my mentality. I have God in me. I have God's wisdom in me. I have God's life in me. That life of God in my spirit dominates me. I purpose in my heart to walk in the light of life."

Now I do not mean that I just skipped by. In study hall periods at school I studied. I listened intently in class to everything that was said. But by receiving eternal life into my spirit, and getting my mind renewed with the Word, my mentality was increased from 30 to 60 percent.

The life of God will do that for anyone.

The most amazing miracle I have ever seen of eternal life affecting someone's mentality occurred in a girl I will call Mary. Her mentality was increased by at least 90 percent.

Mary started to school at seven and went seven years without getting out of the first grade. In those seven years she never learned to write her name. Finally, they asked her parents to take her out of school.

In the church I pastored, Mary was at that time 18 years old, although she behaved like a 2-year-old. She would get down and crawl around on the floor like a baby. If she happened not to be sitting with her mother, she would slide under the pews, or lift up her skirt and step over them to get to where her mother was. Her clothes were always a sight. Her hair was never combed.

Then one night during an evangelistic revival meeting, Mary came to the altar. There she received eternal life — the nature of God. A drastic change occurred instantly. The very next night she sat in the service and behaved like any other 18-year-old young lady. She had fixed her hair and dressed up. Her mentality seemed to have increased overnight.

Years later I was back in the city to help with a funeral. "What ever happened to Mary?" I asked the church secretary. She led me out on the front porch.

"See all those new houses going up out there."

I said, "Yes."

"That's an addition to the city. Mary is building that. She's a widow now. She handles all her own money. She is her own financier. She has three lovely children. They are on the front pew every Sunday. They are the best-dressed, and the most well-mannered children in church. As church secretary I can tell you that Mary's tithes and offerings are here every Sunday."

The life of God came into her!

I am convinced we have never completely learned what we have received. Most of us have thought that the Lord just forgave us, saying that we're the same old creature we always were. We'll just try to hold out faithful till the end. If we get enough people to pray for us, maybe we can make it.

No, thank God, the life of God has been imparted into our spirits! The nature of God is in our spirits. The Holy Spirit is living and abiding in our spirits.

Chapter 13
Two Experiences

Then Philip went down to the city of Samaria,
and preached Christ unto them ... when they
believed Philip preaching the things concerning
the kingdom of God, and the name of Jesus
Christ, they were baptized, both men and
women... Now when the apostles which were
at Jerusalem heard that Samaria had received
the word of God, they sent unto them Peter and
John: Who, when they were come down, prayed
for them, that they might receive the Holy Ghost:
(For as yet he was fallen upon none of them: only
they were baptized in the name of the Lord
Jesus.) Then laid they their hands on them, and
they received the Holy Ghost.

— Acts 8:5,12,14-17

Under the New Covenant every child of God has the
Spirit of God. If you are born again, the Spirit of God is
in your spirit.

We do need to differentiate between being born of the
Spirit and being filled with the Spirit. The born-again
Christian can be *filled* with the same Spirit that he already
has in him. And when he is *filled* with that Spirit, there
will be an overflowing. He will speak with other tongues
as the Spirit gives him utterance (Acts 2:4).

Bible scholars know that water is a type of the Spirit
of God. Jesus Himself used water as a type of the Spirit.
He used it as a type of the new birth when talking to the
woman at the well of Samaria.

JOHN 4:10,11,13,14
10 Jesus answered and said unto her, If thou knewest the
gift of God, and who it is that saith to thee, Give me to

47

drink; thou wouldest have asked of him, and he would have
given thee living water.
11 The woman saith unto him, Sir, thou hast nothing to
draw with, and the well is deep: from whence then hast thou
that living water?
13 Jesus answered and said unto her, Whosoever drinketh
of this water shall thirst again:
14 But whosoever drinketh of the water that I shall give
him shall never thirst; but the water that I shall give him
shall be in him a well of water springing up into everlasting
life.

Jesus also used water as a type of the Spirit in the infilling of the Holy Spirit:

JOHN 7:37-39
37 In the last day, that great day of the feast, Jesus stood
and cried, saying, If any man thirst, let him come unto me,
and drink.
38 He that believeth on me, as the scripture hath said, out
of his belly shall flow rivers of living water.
39 (But this spake he of the Spirit, which they that believe
on him should receive: for the Holy Ghost was not yet
given; because that Jesus was not yet glorified.)

These are two different experiences. The new birth is
a *well of water* in you, springing up into everlasting life.
The infilling of the Holy Spirit is *rivers* — not just one
river. The water in the *well* is for one purpose. The water
in the well is for your own benefit. It blesses you. The water
in the *rivers* is for another purpose. The rivers flowing out
of you bless someone else.

Some people say, "If you are born of the Spirit, you
have the Spirit, and that's all there is." But, no, just
because you have had one drink of water is no sign you're
full of water. There is the experience subsequent to the
new birth of being filled with the Spirit — and as a result,
out of the belly (the innermost being — the spirit) rivers
of living water can flow.

Others say that people who are not filled with the Spirit
speaking with other tongues do not have the Holy Spirit.
That is not true. If I drink half a glass of water, I may
not be full, but at least I have water in me. If one is born
of the Spirit of God, he has the Spirit of God abiding in
him.

Chapter 14
God Inside

... for ye are the temple of the living God; as God hath said, I will dwell in them, and walk in them; and I will be their God, and they shall be my people.   — 2 Corinthians 6:16

If you are born again, the Holy Spirit is living and abiding in your spirit.

He's living and abiding where? In your head? No. In your body? In a sense, yes, but not exactly in the way we might think. The only reason your body becomes the temple of the Holy Spirit is because your body is the temple of your own spirit. The Holy Spirit abides in your *spirit.* And He communicates with you through your spirit.

He does not communicate directly with your mind — He is not in your mind. He is in your spirit — He communicates with you through your spirit. Of course, your spirit does reach and influence your mentality.

Even as a newborn babe in Christ, still bedfast, I would know things by an inward witness. I knew nothing about being filled with the Holy Ghost and speaking with other tongues — but I was born of the Spirit. I had the witness of the Spirit right on the inside of me that I was a child of God.

I had been bedfast about four months when my mother came to my bed one day and said, "Son, I hate to bother you, but something is wrong with Dub."

Dub is my oldest brother. He was 17 at the time and he was gone. We didn't know exactly where he was.

She sensed something in her spirit. She thought maybe he had gotten into trouble and was in jail. She said, "I've been praying for him for three days, but I need some help."

I said, "Momma, I thought you already had enough

problems with me being bedfast. I've known that myself about Dub for several days. He's not in jail, though. It's not that kind of trouble. His physical life is in danger. But I've already prayed, and he will make it. His life will be spared. I've already got the answer."

I didn't know how to get the answer on healing right then — it was a year later before I was healed. But I knew some things, praise God, and God will meet you as far as your faith goes.

Three days later, Dub came home in the nighttime. You see, it was 1933 and there was no work. Men were out on the streets with no jobs in those great Depression Days. Dub had gone down to the Rio Grande Valley to look for work. He didn't find any. So he decided to hop a freight train — lots of people were riding the rails in those days — from the back side of the Valley right on through to McKinney.

About 50 miles south of Dallas a railway detective knocked him in the head and threw him off that train while it was going 50 or 60 miles an hour. He went sailing down the track. They burned coal in those days and they would put the cinders along the track. He hit those cinders and went scooting on his back. It's a wonder it hadn't broken his back. It would have if we hadn't known about it by the inward witness and prayed.

He lay out in the ditch, and then came to after a while. His shirt was completely torn off, and the seat of his britches was torn out, so he could only travel at night. In the daytime he hid out in the trees in the field — it was the time of year he could find fruit — and during the nighttime he walked up the rail toward McKinney. It was night when he got home. Momma put him to bed and he was all right in a few days.

Momma and I were not Spirit-filled Christians — but we were Christians. And we had a witness in our spirits that something was wrong — an inward intuition. This is something every Christian ought to have. It is something every Christian should develop. We should develop our spirits.

In less than ten years' time a Full Gospel minister friend of mine was in three serious automobile accidents. People were killed. His wife was almost killed. He was seriously injured. Cars were demolished. But they were both healed by the mercy of God.

He heard me teach along some of these lines and he said to me, "Brother Hagin, every one of those accidents could have been avoided if I had listened to that inward intuition."

Yet in similar instances people will say, "I don't know why that happened to such a good Christian. He's a preacher." (Preachers have to learn to listen to their spirits just like you have to learn to listen to your spirit.) Then they lay it off on God and say that God did it.

This preacher said to me, "If I had listened to that inward something — I just had an intuition that something was about to happen — I would have waited a little bit and prayed. Instead I thought, *I'm busy. I don't have time to pray.*"

Many times, if we would have waited, God would have shown us. We could have avoided many things. But let's not moan and groan about past failures. Let's just take advantage of what is ours and see to it that it doesn't happen again. We can do nothing about what is past anyhow. Let's begin to develop our spirits, and learn to listen to them.

The Holy Spirit is abiding in your spirit. It is your spirit that picks up these things from the Holy Spirit and then passes them on to your mind by an inward intuition, or inward witness.

Jesus said, "*. . . If a man love me, he will keep my*

words: *and my Father will love him, and we will come unto
him, and make our abode with him"* (John 14:23). In this
passage of scripture, Jesus is talking about the Holy
Spirit's coming. Jesus and the Father in the Person of the
Holy Spirit come to abide in us. An abode is the place
where one lives. Another translation says, "We will come
unto him, and make our home with him."

The Holy Spirit, through the Apostle Paul said, *"Know
ye not that ye are the temple of God, and that the Spirit
of God dwelleth in you?"* (1 Cor. 3:16). Another translation says, "The Spirit of God is at home in you." That's
where He lives — in you!

The Bible says, *". . . for ye are the temple of the living
God; as God hath said, I will dwell in them, and walk in
them; and I will be their God, and they shall be my people"*
(2 Cor. 6:16).

Put those three scriptures together:

**JOHN 14:23; 1 CORINTHIANS 3:16;
2 CORINTHIANS 6:16**
Jesus answered and said unto him, If a man love me, he
will keep my words: and my Father will love him, and we
will come unto him, and make our abode with him . . . Know
ye not that ye are the temple of God, and that the Spirit
of God dwelleth in you? . . . for ye are the temple of the
living God; as God hath said, I will dwell in them, and walk
in them; and I will be their God, and they shall be my
people.

We have never yet plumbed the depth of what God is
really saying: "I will dwell in them. I will live in them. I
will walk in them." If God is dwelling *in* us — and He is —
then that is where He will speak to us.

Chapter 15
Depend on Your Spirit

*For verily I say unto you, That whosoever
shall say unto this mountain, Be thou removed,
and be thou cast into the sea; and shall not doubt
in his heart, but shall believe that those things
which he saith shall come to pass; he shall have
whatsoever he saith. Therefore I say unto you,
What things soever ye desire, when ye pray,
believe that ye receive them, and ye shall have
them.* — Mark 11:23,24

Your spirit knows things that your head does not know,
because the Holy Spirit is in your spirit.

When medical science gave me up to die as a teenager
and said they could do nothing further for me, I knew
somehow that if there was help for me anywhere it would
be in the Bible.

I started with the New Testament because I knew I
didn't have much time. Eventually I came to Mark 11:23
and 24.

When I came to Mark 11:24, something from outside
me somewhere said to my mind, *That doesn't mean what
things soever ye desire physically, or materially, or finan-
cially. That just means whatsoever things ye desire
spiritually. Healing has been done away with.*

I tried to get my pastor to come and tell me what Mark
11:24 did mean. He did not come. One preacher finally did
come. He patted my hand, put on a professional voice and
said, "Just be patient my boy. In a few more days it will
all be over."

I accepted the verdict and lay there expecting to die.
It was two months before I got back into the Bible and
back to Mark 11:23 and 24.

I said, "Lord, I tried to get someone to help me and I couldn't. So I am going to tell You what I am going to do. I am just going to take You at Your Word. When You were here on earth, You said it. I am going to believe it. If You didn't lie about it, I am coming off this bed, because I can believe what You said I can believe."

Then I hit on this idea. (It took me a long time because I had limited use of my hands. They propped the Bible in front of me and I just sort of "scooted" the pages.) I decided to run my reference on *faith* and *healing*. I came to James 5:14 and 15.

> **JAMES 5:14,15**
> 14 Is any sick among you? let him call for the elders of the church; and let them pray over him, anointing him with oil in the name of the Lord:
> 15 And the prayer of faith shall save the sick, and the Lord shall raise him up; and if he have committed sins, they shall be forgiven him.

I thought all the rest of the healing scriptures and prayer promises hinged on that — I thought you HAD to call for the elders of the church. (You don't have to — you just can if you need to.) So I began to cry, "Dear Lord, if I have to call for the elders of the church to anoint me with oil to be healed, then I can't be healed. I don't know any elders of the church that believe in that."

I had been saved about six months, and I had never heard an inward voice. I am not talking about the voice of the Spirit of God — that is more authoritative — I am talking about that still small voice of my spirit.

My spirit said to me, "Did you notice that verse said that the prayer of faith shall save the sick?"

I had to look again. I'd had my mind on the elders and had missed that. "Yes," I said aloud, "that is what it says!" It came as a real shock to me.

Then on the inside of me these words were spoken, "You can pray that prayer as well as anyone can." Hallelujah!

But my spiritual education was slow — just like yours. I stayed in that bed nine more months before I finally saw that I had to believe I received my healing before it would be manifested.

It was while I was praying and saying, "I believe that I receive my healing," that I saw what I must do. I said, "I believe that I receive healing from the top of my head to the soles of my feet." Then I began to praise God because I believed that I received my healing.

Again, on the inside of me, I heard these words — this was not that authoritative voice, but just a still small voice, so faint I would not have heard it if my mind and body had been very active — "Now you believe that you are well."

I said, "I sure do."

That inward voice said, "Get up then. Well people ought to be up at 10:30 in the morning."

I had been paralyzed. It was a struggle. I pushed myself. Finally, I got up to where I was draped over the bedpost. My knees sagged down not far from the floor. I had no feeling from my waist down. But draped over that bedpost I said it again, "I want to announce in the Presence of Almighty God, the Lord Jesus Christ, the Holy Spirit, and the holy angels present in this room, and I want to call the devil to record and all evil spirits that may be present in this room, that according to Mark 11:24, I believe that I receive my healing."

When I said that, physically, I felt something. It felt like someone above me was pouring a pitcher of honey on me. I felt it strike me on the top of my head. It seemed to pile up like honey would, and then it began to ooze down over me. It had a warm glow to it. It spread down over my head, down my neck and shoulders, down my arms and out the ends of my fingers, and down my body and out the ends of my toes.

All of a sudden I was standing straight! I have been straight ever since.

But I want you to see this. I listened to my spirit. Faith is of the spirit. Your faith will not work to its fullest until you learn some of these things. Learn to depend on Him — the One who is in you. Learn to develop your own spirit. Have faith in the fact that *your* faith in God works.

Chapter 16
Tenderhearted

For if our heart condemn us, God is greater
than our heart, and knoweth all things. Beloved,
if our heart condemn us not, then have we con-
fidence toward God.   — 1 John 3:20,21

Does the Holy Spirit condemn you if you do wrong as
a Christian?

No. It is your spirit that condemns you.

You need to learn that. It's a hard lesson to learn,
however, because we have been taught incorrectly.

The Holy Spirit will not condemn you. Why? Because
God won't. Study what the Holy Spirit through Paul wrote
in the Epistle to the Romans. He asked: Who is it that
condemns? Does God condemn? No, it is God that
justifies.

Jesus said that the only sin the Holy Spirit will con-
vict the world of is the sin of rejecting Jesus (John 16:7-9).

It is your own conscience — the voice of your own
spirit — that knows when you have done wrong.

I have found that even when I do wrong, though my
spirit condemns me, the Holy Spirit is there to comfort
me, to help me, to show me the way back. You will never
read in the Bible where the Holy Spirit is a condemner.
Jesus called Him *the Comforter.* The seven-fold meaning
of that word from the Greek is brought out in *The
Amplified Bible:*

JOHN 14:16 *Amplified*
**16 And I will ask the Father, and He will give you another
Comforter (Counselor, Helper, Intercessor, Advocate,
Strengthener and Standby) that He may remain with you
forever.**

The Holy Spirit is all of those! He will stand by you

when no one else will. He will help you. He is a Helper!

It is your own spirit that knows the moment you have done wrong. I am glad I learned that early. It has paid off richly for me in life.

I was barely saved and healed and back in high school when the following incident occurred: I really don't know why it slipped out — no one in our family used profanity. But we had a neighbor, bless his heart, who could — as we say in Texas — "cuss up a storm." You could hear him all over our end of town. I suppose I picked it up from him. Anyway, I simply said to one of the boys, "Hell, no . . . (something or other)."

The minute I said that I knew on the inside it was wrong. What was it that condemned me? the Holy Spirit? No. It was my spirit. My spirit, this new creature, this new man doesn't talk that way. The Life and Nature of God doesn't talk that way. Now the flesh, the outward man, may want to go on doing some things that he did before, and talking in ways he talked before, but you have to crucify the flesh. A good way to crucify the flesh — the outward man — is to bring your mistakes right out in the open.

I did that right then. I didn't wait until I was moved. In my heart I said, "Dear God, forgive me for saying that." The young man I said it to had walked away. I located him and asked him to forgive me. He hadn't noticed what I'd said; he was used to people talking that way. But I had to get it right.

It was the voice of my spirit. It was my conscience. My conscience was tender, and I didn't want to violate it. *Unless you keep a tender conscience, spiritual things will be indistinct to you.* That's because your conscience is the voice of your spirit and it is your conscience — the voice of your spirit — that will relate to your mind what the Spirit of God is saying to you down in your heart.

The Bible speaks about Christians even having their conscience seared:

1 TIMOTHY 4:2
2 Speaking lies in hypocrisy; having their conscience seared with a hot iron.

The first church I pastored was a community church out in the country. I usually went out Saturday night, spent Saturday and Sunday nights, and came back into town on Monday. I stayed quite often in the home of a dear Methodist man. This fine spiritual man, a great man really, was 89 years old. He and I didn't get up as early as the others did on his farm. They would be out doing chores or be out working in the field when this older gentleman and I had breakfast together about 8 o'clock.

I didn't drink coffee, but this old gentleman did. Now you could scarcely believe it unless you saw it, but he had one of those old-fashioned coffee pots — this was the mid-30's — sitting on an old-fashioned wood stove with coffee boiling in it. I have seen him take that boiling coffee, pour it into a big thick mug — and when it was still so hot it simmered in that mug — turn it up to his mouth, and drink the whole cup.

The first time I saw him do it, I hollered. I felt like my mouth and throat were burning.

How could he do that? I couldn't. The tissues of my lips, the inside of my mouth, my throat and esophagus are so tender, just one teaspoonful would have burned all the way down. But he drank a whole mug without taking it away from his mouth.

He couldn't do that to begin with though. Through years of drinking coffee that hot, his lips and mouth, and throat and esophagus became seared. Eventually, he could drink it that hot, and it didn't bother him.

Spiritually, the same thing can happen.

Learn to keep a tender conscience. Learn the minute you miss it and your conscience condemns you, to correct it right then. Don't wait until you go to church. Immediately say, "Lord, forgive me. I missed it." If you have to, if someone else saw or heard you, tell that person right away, "I did wrong. Please forgive me. I shouldn't have said that."

You will have to keep your spirit tender if you are going to be led by the Spirit.

Chapter 17
Feelings:
The Voice of the Body

The Spirit itself [Himself] *beareth witness*
with our spirit....   — Romans 8:16

Too often people think that the witness this verse is
talking about is a physical something. It is not. It is a
spiritual something. It is the Spirit of God bearing witness
with our spirits. He does not bear witness with our bodies.
You cannot go by physical feeling.

We confuse things by the way we talk. We say, "I *feel*
God's Presence." No, we don't. We sense His Presence
spiritually. Use the word *feeling* advisedly; it leaves the
wrong impression that it is a physical feeling. Don't mix
the physical with it.

Feeling is the voice of the body.

Reason is the voice of the soul, or the mind.

Conscience is the voice of the spirit.

To go by *feeling* is to get into trouble. That is the reason
so many Christians are up and down (I call them yo-yo
Christians), and in and out. They go by their feelings. They
don't walk by faith. They don't walk by their spirits.

When they feel good, they say, "Glory to God, I'm
saved. Hallelujah, I'm filled with the Spirit. Everything
is fine." When they feel bad, their faces are long and they
say, "I've lost it all. I don't feel like I did, so I must be
backslidden."

I hear people, bless their hearts, talking about being
in the valley, then being on the mountaintop, then getting
back down in the valley again. I have never been in the
valley. I have been saved more than fifty years and I have
never been anywhere but on the mountaintop. You do not
have to get down in the valley.

People talk about "valley experiences." I have never had any valley experiences. Oh, yes, there have been tests and trials, but I was on the mountaintop all the time, shouting my way through — living above the tests and the trials!

A woman we had pastored in years gone by came to a meeting where we were and told us about her 39-year-old daughter. They were about to operate on her when they discovered she had a tumor. Then they also found through hospital tests that she was a diabetic. They were trying to get the diabetic condition under control when she went into a coma. Three doctors said she would never regain consciousness; she would die.

This mother said, "Will you lay your hands on this handkerchief?" I did, and we prayed. Then that mother got on a bus and rode 300 miles back to the hospital where her daughter lay unconscious. She reached under the oxygen tent and laid the handkerchief on her daughter's chest. The minute it touched her, she revived. She was healed, born again, filled with the Holy Spirit and began to speak in tongues, all in one application.

The nurses got excited and called the doctor. The doctor said, "This is wonderful that she has regained consciousness. But she must remain quiet." He gave her a shot to quieten her down — but it never did take effect. She just kept on speaking in tongues and shouting, "I'm healed. I'm healed. I'm healed."

The next day they began to run tests. Her blood was perfect. She no longer had diabetes. Then they couldn't find the tumor. It had disappeared. After several days they dismissed her.

This woman told my wife and me sometime later that the doctor said, "We won't charge you anything. We didn't do anything. A Higher Power than us did it."

Now, three years later, when she was 42 years old, her

sister brought her to our door at 2 o'clock one morning. She had another tumor.

I thought she had come to be healed. So I said, "You can be healed again. We will just lay hands on you."

She said, with tears, "Brother Hagin, I don't really care whether I get healed or not. Really, if I could just get back to where I was with God I would just as soon die and go on to Heaven."

When she said this, I assumed she must have backslidden. She looked so sad, I just knew she must have committed some terrible sin. So I said, "The Lord will forgive you . . ." And I went through what the Bible says about that. Then I said, "We'll all just kneel down here by the couch. (My wife and the woman's sister were there too.) I will kneel beside you. Now you don't have to confess to me, but tell the Lord about it and He will forgive you."

She looked up at me and said, "Brother Hagin, I've searched my heart, and as far as I know, I haven't done anything wrong."

I got aggravated. I'd gotten to bed late — I was driving a distance and holding meetings every night. And just right in the middle of good sound sleep, early in the morning, came this knocking at the door that woke us. I guess I did speak sharply to her; I know I did.

I said, "Get up from the floor. Sit down there on that couch." I was disgusted. "If you haven't done anything wrong, what in the world makes you think you have to get back to God?"

"Well," she said, "I don't *feel* like I used to."

I said, "What has that got to do with it? If I were going by feeling, half the time when I get up to preach I would announce that I must be backslidden."

She looked at me. "Do you mean preachers are that way too?"

I said, "Yes, we're just as human as anyone else. In

fact, if I were going by feelings right now, I would be having you pray for me. I don't feel a thing. I haven't felt a thing since you got here."

She said, "What do you do then? How do you pray through?"

I said, "I don't pray through. I'm already through. A Christian ought to walk through — he ought to be *through* — living in fellowship with God, every day, every minute, every hour."

She said, "What do you do then?"

"Well," I said, "just sit there and watch me. I'm going to close my eyes and pray, but you keep your eyes open."

Then I prayed, "Dear Lord, I'm so glad that I'm a child of God. I'm so glad I'm saved. I'm so glad I have been born again. I don't feel anything — but that has nothing to do with it. My inward man is a new man. My inward man is a new creature in Christ. I want to thank You that not only am I born again — but I am filled with the Holy Spirit. God the Father, God the Son, and God the Holy Spirit reside in me. I want to thank You for that. Hallelujah!"

I didn't feel anything, but I said it anyhow. Then, when I confessed that, in my spirit (He was in there all the time) something began to bubble up inside of me. It was a move and manifestation of the Spirit of God. I still did not feel anything, but in my spirit I could sense that bubbling. It got up in my throat. I began to laugh — there is a laugh in the Spirit. I began to speak in tongues.

This lady said, "The expression on your face changed. Your face just lit up."

I said, "That was in there all the time. Paul told Timothy to stir up the gift that was in him. I just stirred up what I had in me all the time."

She said, "Can I do that?"

I said, "Yes, you can."

She did — she stirred up what was in her all the time.

I do not remember even praying about the tumor. The last account I had of her, it had disappeared.

Base your faith on the Word — not on your feelings.

Romans 8:16 does not say that the Spirit beareth witness with our bodies, or with our feelings.

Smith Wigglesworth, the great English apostle of faith, said, "I am not moved by what I feel. I am not moved by what I see. I am moved only by what I believe. I cannot understand God by feelings. I understand God by what the Word says about Him. I understand the Lord Jesus Christ by what the Word says about Him. He is everything the Word says He is."

You cannot understand yourself by feelings. Understand yourself as a born-again, Spirit-filled Christian by what the Word of God says about you. And when you read what the Word says about you — then, whether you feel like it or not, say, "Yes, that's me. I have that. The Word says I have that. I can do what the Word says I can do. I am what the Word says I am."

You will begin to develop spiritually then.

And it is with your spirit that the Holy Spirit bears witness.

Chapter 18
Help From Within

*Howbeit when he, the Spirit of truth, is come,
he will guide you into all truth: for he shall not
speak of himself; but whatsoever he shall hear,
that shall he speak: and he will shew you things
to come.*   — John 16:13

Let's notice some things Jesus said about the Holy
Spirit in John 16:13. "*. . . he will guide you into all
truth. . . .*" He will lead you. He will guide you.

"*. . . for he shall not speak of himself; but whatsoever
he shall hear, that shall he speak. . . .*" The Holy Spirit does
speak. Whatever He hears God say, whatever He hears
Jesus say, He will speak to your spirit. Where is He to
speak? He is in your spirit, and that is where He speaks.
He doesn't speak out in the air somewhere. He speaks on
the inside. The Holy Spirit passes God's message on to
your spirit, either by an inward witness, by the still small
voice — the voice of your conscience, or by an inward voice
which is the more authoritative voice of the Holy Spirit.

"*. . . he will shew you things to come. . . .*" I do not
believe this just means that the Holy Spirit will show us
about future events as recorded in the Word of God. It
also means that the Holy Spirit will show *you* things to
come. In my own individual life, for instance, there has
never been a death in our close family that I did not
know about in advance. I knew two years ahead of time
that my father-in-law was going to die, so I began to
prepare my wife for his death. She was his only daughter,
the baby of the family, and very close to her father. I knew
she would take it hard. So I began to say to her, "Honey,
you know Mr. Rooker is getting older. Then over the next
two years I dropped a word here and there, just getting

her ready.

I was away in a meeting when the telephone call came. After the service one night, I was sitting in the hotel. The phone rang. Something in me said, "That's for you. This is what you have been talking about for two years now." Within twenty-eight days he was in Heaven. You are not unprepared when you know things ahead of time.

> **JOHN 14:26**
> **26 But the Comforter, which is the Holy Ghost, whom the Father will send in my name, he shall teach you all things, and bring all things to your remembrance, whatsoever I have said unto you.**

The Holy Spirit shall teach you.

He shall bring all things to your remembrance.

People often ask me how I remember things. At one time I could quote three-fourths of the New Testament.

"How do you memorize scripture?"

I always answer, "I never memorized scripture in my life. I know nothing about memorization. I suppose you could develop your mind if you worked at it. But I just get to talking and it rises up in me. The Holy Spirit brings it to my remembrance. He is inside of me."

The Holy Spirit will show you things to come and bring things to your remembrance if you will learn to cooperate with Him.

Chapter 19
Number Three:
The Voice of the Holy Spirit

*While Peter thought on the vision, the Spirit
said unto him, Behold, three men seek thee.*
— Acts 10:19

God leads us by what we call the still small voice. But
He also leads us by the voice of the Spirit of God speaking to us. This is the third way we are led by the Spirit.
Number one is by the inward witness. Number two is by
the inward still small voice. Number three is by the more
authoritative voice of the Holy Spirit.

There is a difference between the inward voice of the
Holy Spirit speaking to our spirits, and that still small
voice which is the voice of our own spirit speaking to us.
When the Holy Spirit within you speaks, it is more
authoritative.

Sometimes it is so real it almost seems to be an audible
voice; you may even look around to see who said it. It may
seem so audible sometimes that you may think someone
behind you said something. But then you realize it was
in you.

Remember in the Old Testament how the young boy
Samuel heard a voice call his name, "Samuel, Samuel?"
He thought Eli was calling him. He jumped up and ran
to Eli to find out what he wanted. Eli said, "No, I didn't
call you." Samuel went back to bed. Then again he heard,
"Samuel, Samuel." Again he ran to Eli. "No, I didn't call
you." It happened the third time. Finally, it dawned on
Eli what was happening. Eli said, "The next time the Lord
calls you, answer Him." So the next time it happened,
Samuel answered that voice, and the Lord spoke further
to him (1 Sam. Chapter 3).

All of God's leadings are supernatural; some, however, are not so spectacular. But I have found in more than fifty years of ministry that when God moved in a more spectacular way — when He has spoken to me in what seemed to me to be an audible voice — it meant there was rough sailing ahead. If He had not spoken so spectacularly I would not have stayed steady.

Concerning the last church I pastored, for example, I heard the pastorate was open and I made arrangements to preach there one Wednesday night. During the period of time before I was to go there to preach, I held a three-week revival in Houston. During this revival, the pastor, his brother (who was also a preacher), and I met at the church every day to pray about the night services. The church with the open pastorate was their home church. Every day the pastor and his brother would ask me, "Have you prayed about that church yet?"

Finally, I did pray about it. I just said to the Lord, "I'm going up to that church next Monday and I'm going to preach Wednesday. I don't know whether You want me to pastor there or not. I don't know if I even want to pastor it. But whatever You say about it is fine with me."

That is all I said. Then I heard a voice speak so plainly, I jumped. I looked behind me. I really thought that one of the preachers had heard me pray and was joking with me, because I heard this voice, and to me it was audible. The voice said, "You are the next pastor at that church, and that will be the last church you will ever pastor."

(You could interpret that a thousand different ways! You could let the devil tell you that you were going to die, or that you were going to be defeated. But it actually meant that my ministry would change to a field ministry.)

About then those two preachers walked down the aisle. As usual, they asked, "Have you prayed about that church yet?"

I said, "You two fellows are looking at the next pastor."

"Oooh, if you knew that church like we know it, you wouldn't say that. It's split right down the middle. Anything half the church is for, the other half is against. It takes two-thirds of the vote to get elected as pastor, and we'll just be honest with you, you won't be able to get elected."

"I don't know about that. I just know I'm the next pastor."

"Well, you don't know that church like we do."

I said, "No, but I know Jesus. And I know the Spirit of God. I know what He said to me."

After I preached the first time, I saw why God moved in such a spectacular way. Every word I spoke bounced right back to me like a rubber ball bouncing off the back wall. It was tough.

I thought I was only going to preach one night, but they had made arrangements for me to preach several nights. Each night my wife and children and I had to move to a different place to stay. We were at one deacon's house one night, and another deacon's house the next night.

One deacon told us, "If you stayed with me all the time, some of the rest of the congregation would probably get jealous and think I'm for you and they would vote against you."

We kept all our things in the car, and every night we would get out just enough for the next day. And every night when we got off to bed, I would say to my wife, "If God hadn't spoken so spectacularly to me, I would just get up, get the children, get into the car, and leave without saying a word to anyone."

My flesh wanted to leave so badly. My mind wanted to leave. My spirit held me steady because God had spoken to me in such a spectacular way.

They had the election. I got every vote. Everyone said,

"It's the greatest miracle of the century — that anyone could get that kind of vote from this church."

I knew all the time I would get it. The Spirit of God had told me I would.

Chapter 20
Judging By the Word

Prove all things. . . .— 1 Thessalonians 5:21

Always remember this: the Bible teaches that the Spirit of God and the Word of God agree. Anytime the Spirit of God speaks to you, it will always be in line with the Word.

People have heard "voices" and have gotten every kind of "revelation" you can imagine. Some people are always claiming to hear a voice.

You can, and you should, judge these things. You can judge whether spiritual experiences are right or wrong simply by judging them by the Word.

Several years ago I was preaching in California. A woman who had invited the pastor, his wife, and me to her home for the noon meal said, "Brother Hagin, I want to tell you what the Lord said to me. I want to give you my *revelation.*"

Before she opened her mouth I sensed by the inward witness in my spirit that something was not right. But she persisted, and I agreed to listen. She had fed us in her lovely home, and now she wanted to give me this "revelation." She began to relate it and she talked for about ten minutes before I stopped her. I just couldn't stand anymore.

"Please," I said, "wait a minute. There's a Bible there on the table by the chair. Pick it up and open it to _____." I gave her a chapter and verse in the New Testament. "Read that."

She read it. Then I gave her another verse of scripture. She read it. I pointed her to several scriptures. Everything she read contradicted what she said.

I said, "See, I cannot accept what you are saying. It

75

is not in line with this Book. Therefore it cannot be the Spirit of God."

"But, Brother Hagin, I was praying at the altar."

I said, "I don't care if you were praying on top of the church. It's still not right. It is not in line with the Word."

"Yes, but I know God gave this to me."

I said, "No, He didn't. This is His Word and what you are saying is in direct opposition to what the Word of God says. Can you give me any scripture to substantiate what you are saying?"

"No. But I know I heard this voice speak to me."

"I just gave you five scriptures, and with a little thought I could have given you twenty, that contradict what you are saying."

"Well, yes," she said, "but Bible or no Bible, I know God spoke to me and I am going to stay with it."

As we left, the pastor said to me, "I didn't want to say anything to you before, but this dear woman was a fine saint of God, on fire for the Lord. She was a blessing to the church. Now she has been put out of every Full Gospel church in the city because she persists in pushing this *revelation* off on everyone."

We are not to seek voices.

We should not follow voices.

We should follow the Word of God.

I preached a meeting in Oregon in the summer of 1954. At the close of one of the first services, I was laying hands on the people who stood in the long prayer line. I asked each one what they had come forward for before I ministered to them. When I came to one woman, her husband who had her by the arm said, "We have come for my wife's healing." He told me she'd had a mental breakdown.

I did not know this woman was a former Sunday School teacher in that church, nor that her husband was a deacon in the church.

But when I laid hands on her, in a second of time just like it ran off on a television screen, I knew all about this situation. I knew it by the spiritual gift called the word of knowledge (1 Cor. 12:8). I saw this woman in a large tent meeting in one of Oregon's largest cities. I saw her sitting in the congregation with thousands of people. She heard the evangelist tell how God spoke to him in an audible voice and called him into the ministry.

I do not doubt that. This woman failed to realize, however, that this evangelist did not ask God to speak to him that way. God just did it on His own. We have no right to seek that God would speak to us in an audible voice. If God told us He would in His Word, then all of us would have a right to claim it. But this evangelist hadn't even particularly expected God to speak in that way — but if God wants to, He can, and He saw fit to do so in that particular case.

At the time this woman heard the evangelist tell that, she was all right mentally. But then she began to seek God to speak to her in an audible voice — and the devil accommodated her. She began to hear voices. They drove her insane. She was now about to be taken to the asylum for the second time.

I also saw this in the spirit: Her husband had taken her to this same evangelist for deliverance. She did not receive deliverance. Now her husband blamed that evangelist. Then her husband had taken her to another leading evangelist. She had failed to be delivered. Now her husband was angry with that other evangelist too. I knew she would not be delivered if I laid hands on her, and then he would be angry with me. So I took my hand off of her.

I said to the man, "Take your wife into the pastor's study. Wait there. When I finish this line, I will talk with you."

After we were finished with the healing line, the pastor and I went into the study together.

"First of all," I said to this couple, "I have never been to Oregon before. I have never seen you folks before. I don't even know if the pastor knows you."

The pastor said, "He's one of our deacons."

"Well," I said, "the pastor will tell you he has not told me anything."

Then I related what I had seen.

The deacon said, "That's exactly right."

"Now," I said, "I will tell you why I didn't minister to your wife. You see, she wants to hear these voices."

Then I said, "She is not that far gone mentally that she doesn't know what I am saying."

She spoke up, "I know exactly what you are saying."

I said, "Sister, you are not going to be delivered until you want to be delivered. As long as you like it the way it is — as long as you want to hear these voices — you are going to hear them."

She said, "I want to hear them."

As long as a sinner wants to live in sin, God will let him live in sin. But if he wants to change, God will meet him and deliver him.

And even though a person is a Christian, that does not mean he loses his free moral agency. He does not become a robot — a machine whereby God pushes a button and he automatically has to do whatever God desires. He is still a free moral agent. As long as he wants things like they are, they will stay that way. But if he wants to cooperate with God, he can be helped.

This woman said, "That's the way I want it."

I said, "I knew that the minute I touched you. That's the reason I didn't minister to you. As long as you want it this way, it's going to be this way."

DO NOT SEEK VOICES!

1 CORINTHIANS 14:10
10 There are, it may be, so many kinds of voices in the world, and none of them is without signification.

We are not to accept anything without examining it in the light of the Word of God.

I am glad that I learned some of these things early in life. I mentioned I received my healing as a young boy by just acting on Mark 11:23 and 24.

I was born with a deformed heart. I never ran and played as other children did. I became bedfast four months before my sixteenth birthday. My body became practically totally paralyzed. I wasted away until I weighed only 89 pounds.

One day I asked the fifth doctor on the case, "Is something wrong with my eyesight, or with my blood? When Dr. Mathis took blood from my finger, it didn't look red."

This doctor said, "I will tell you the truth, son. And I will explain it to you in layman's terms. The white blood corpuscles eat up the red corpuscles faster than you can build them up, or we, medically, can do anything about it. If you didn't have the heart condition, if you didn't have the paralysis, this incurable blood disease alone would prove fatal."

I knew nothing about divine healing. I didn't know anyone in all the world believed in divine healing. When I found it in the Bible, I thought I had found something no one else knew anything about. And I acted on God's Word and was healed.

The members of my family were what we call *nominal* Christians. Literally, they were baby Christians. They were saved, but they were not taught beyond that. They were ignorant of the Word of God concerning healing. (Our church taught God could heal, if He *would*. Others taught not only that He *would* not heal, but that He *could* not heal.) So when I began to see certain things in the Bible and began to talk to my family about them, they discouraged me. I had enough sense just to stay with the Bible and keep those things to myself.

No one was in the room when I received my healing. I had been getting up and walking around the room for a couple of days before I said to Momma, "Please bring me a pair of shoes and socks, some underclothes, and a pair of pants and a shirt. (I had worn nothing but bedclothes for 16 months.) I am going to get up and go to the breakfast table in the morning."

"Oh, son, do you know what you're doing?"

It took me 45 minutes to talk her into the notion of laying out those clothes for me.

We made our home with my grandparents on my mother's side, and I asked my mother not to tell the rest of the family.

Now you could just mark it down. Grandpa got up early and sat out on the porch swing. When you heard that porch swing creak as he got up and headed toward the back of the house to the dining room, there was no use in looking at your watch; it was 7:30. Grandpa ran on schedule. If you did look at your watch, and it didn't say 7:30, you had better set it. It was 7:30.

My bedroom was in the front of the house. At 7:30 that August morning I heard that porch swing creak. I heard his footsteps as he walked to the back of the house. I was already fully clothed, sitting in a chair in my room. I gave them time to get seated at the table. Then I walked out of my room, across another bedroom, and into the dining room.

They did not expect that. Grandpa, a man of few words, looked up and said, "Is the dead raised? Is Lazarus raised up?"

I said, "Yes, the Lord has raised me up."

Then he asked me to offer the blessing. I prayed. And we ate. It is amazing how quickly you can eat if you don't talk so much. You didn't talk at Grandpa's table — especially the young folks. Within 15 minutes we were finished.

I went back to my room. It was ten minutes till 8 o'clock. I knew Momma would come in about 8 o'clock to make up the bed. Usually I was in it and she would give me my bath. Just two days before, the day I was healed, she had bathed me. I was that helpless. So this Thursday morning, even though my heart was beating right, I felt weak from exerting so much energy.

So I thought, *I'm just going to lie down across the bed and rest till Momma comes to clean the room. Then I'll go out and sit with Grandpa in the swing.* I had in mind to walk uptown about 10 o'clock.

I dozed off to sleep and slept ten minutes. At 8 o'clock I suddenly became wide awake. I thought Momma was in the room. Someone was in the room. I didn't see him, but I heard this voice — to me it was audible.

The voice spoke in a slow, deep monotone and even quoted scripture. It said, "AND WHAT IS YOUR LIFE? IT IS EVEN A VAPOR THAT APPEARETH FOR A TIME, AND THEN VANISHETH AWAY."

There was a pause.

Then the voice said, "AND TODAY THOU SHALT SURELY DIE."

Every voice is not God. The first audible voice I ever heard was the devil, but I didn't recognize that then. I thought God was right there in that room.

I sat up in the bed. Thoughts came into my mind faster than machine gun bullets fly. I knew James said, *"For what is your life? It is even a vapour, that appeareth for a little time, and then vanisheth away"* (James 4:14). I

knew that was scripture. And I knew the Lord told Isaiah
to tell Hezekiah, *"Set thine house in order: for thou shalt
die, and not live"* (Isa. 38:1).

Also, for the first six months of being bedfast, before
I had known about divine healing, I had prayed the only
way I understood. The doctors had said I had to die and
I had accepted it, so I had prayed, "Lord, just let me know
ahead of time, so I will have time to tell everyone good-
bye."

So when I heard this voice speaking to me, I thought
*God has moved in this supernatural way to let you know
you are going to die so you will have time to tell everyone
good-bye. Divine healing is right. You have been healed.*
(The devil couldn't argue that. I already had the Word on
that.) *Your family knows you have been healed. They can
see that. But remember, the Bible said, "It is appointed
unto men once to die," and your appointed time has come.
You are going to die today."*

I got up off the bed and I tiptoed across the room (I
thought God was standing right in that room) and I sat
down in a chair by the window. There I waited, from about
8:30 in the morning until 2:30 in the afternoon, to die.

About 2:30, still sitting in that chair, some words came
floating up from somewhere down inside me. I didn't know
then what I know now. But I was born of the Spirit. The
Holy Spirit was in my spirit. And He is the One who wrote
the Bible. Holy men of old wrote as they were moved by
the Spirit of God. The Holy Spirit knows what is in that
Book. Because He was in me, then my spirit knew some
things that the Holy Spirit knows.

So these words came floating up from somewhere inside
me into my mind, *With long life will I satisfy him, and
show him my salvation.*

I didn't listen to them. I just let them float away from
me. I still sat there waiting to die.

The second time, these words came floating up from inside me into my mind, *With long life will I satisfy him, and show him my salvation.*

I picked them up and turned them over a couple of times in my mind. Then I thought, *Yes, but God has moved in this supernatural way to let me know I am going to die today.* When I got my mind on that, those words disappeared.

The third time, as I sat there and these words came floating up, that inward something said to my mind, *With long life will I satisfy him, and show him my salvation.*

For a moment, I picked them up and repeated them just in my mind. Then I said, in a whisper, "Yes, but God has moved in this supernatural way to let me know that I am going to die." Again, when I got my mind on that, I missed it.

The fourth time, a little more authoritatively, the Spirit of God spoke. I jumped. I thought someone had slipped up behind me. The voice of the Spirit of God said, "With long life will I satisfy him, and show him my salvation."

I said, "Who said that?" I meant, Who is in this room talking to me?

But the voice answered and said, "The 91st Psalm."

My Bible was on the floor under the chair I had been sitting in all day. I hadn't even looked at it. I picked it up now and turned to Psalm 91. When I got down to the end, sure enough, it said, *"With long life will I satisfy him, and shew him my salvation"* (v. 16).

But do you think the devil will give up that quickly? Oh, no. Another voice — it seemed like something sitting on my shoulder — said in my natural ear and mind, "Yes, but that's in the Old Testament. That's just for the Jews. That's not for the Church."

I sat there and thought for a moment. Then I said, "I know what I'll do. I will run my references. If I can find anything in the New Testament like that I will know it belongs to me and to the Church.''

I started with Psalm 91. A reference to "with long life" led me into Proverbs. Then the Word began to enlighten me. In Proverbs I began to see that that first audible voice could not have been God.

The voice had quoted Hebrews 9:27, *"And as it is appointed unto men once to die, but after this the judgment,"* but had misinterpreted it. Because the devil knew I didn't know any better, the voice had said, "Everyone has an appointed time to die." You hear people say that all the time. Even born-again, Spirit-filled Christians say, "When your time comes, you're going to die." That is not true. You do not have an appointed time to die.

I read in the Book of Proverbs again and again that if you do certain things, your days will be shortened. But doing other things will add unto you length of days. I knew God's Word was right. I knew that even though that voice picked a verse out of a chapter and gave it to me, it could not have been God, because it was not in line with the rest of the Word of God.

I continued to run references. This brought me over into the New Testament. I came over to Ephesians 6:1-3. And then into First and Second Peter. And I found that Paul and Peter quoted the Old Testament concerning long life (1 Peter 3:8-12; 2 Peter 1:3).

I jumped up out of that chair with my Bible in one hand. I doubled up my fist, kicked with my foot, and said, "Devil, you get out of here. That was you talking to me. That was you that spoke to me in that supernatural voice. I want you to know that I'm not going to die today! And I'm not going to die tomorrow! And I'm not going to die next week! And I'm not going to die next month! And I'm not going to die next year! And I'm not going to die the next 5 years! And I'm not going to die the next 10 years!

And I'm not going to die the next 15 years! And I'm not
going to die the next 20 years! And I'm not going to die
the next 25 years! And I'm not going to die the next 30
years! And I'm not going to die the next 40 years! And
I'm not going to die the next 50 years! And I'm not going
to die the next 55 years!

God's Word says, "With long life will I *satisfy* thee"
(Ps. 91:16). And I'm going to go on living until I am
satisfied!

Chapter 21
My Spirit? The Flesh? or
The Holy Spirit?

The spirit of man is the candle of the Lord. . . .
— Proverbs 20:27

Someone might ask, "How can I tell whether it is my own spirit, or the Holy Spirit telling me to do something?"

The spirit of man is the candle of the Lord.

"But it may just be *me* wanting to do it."

Define your terms. If by "me" you mean the flesh, of course you cannot always obey the flesh. But if by "me" you mean the inward man, the real you, then it is all right to obey the inward man. Go ahead and do what he wants you to do.

If your spirit is a new creature in Christ Jesus and old things have passed away and all things are become new, and your spirit has the life and nature of God in it and the Holy Spirit in it, and your spirit is in fellowship with God — it is not going to tell you to do something that is not right. If you are a Spirit-filled Christian, your inward man has the Holy Spirit in His fullness — not in a measure, but in His fullness — making His home in you.

It is not the inward man of the Christian that wants to do wrong — it is the outward man. You ought to be able to tell whether it is the flesh wanting to do something, or the spirit. Here is a text that has been a puzzle to many:

1 JOHN 3:9
9 Whosoever is born of God doth not commit sin; for his seed remaineth in him: and he cannot sin, because he is born of God.

This is talking about the inward man. Physically we are born of human parents and we partake of their nature.

Spiritually we are born of God and partake of His nature. God's nature is not the nature to do wrong.

I have missed it a lot of times as a Christian. But my inward man did not sin. He didn't even agree with me when I did sin. He tried to get me not to do it. My heart wept because I sinned. I allowed my flesh to dominate and I missed it, but my spirit never did consent to it. God's seed is in my spirit, not in my flesh.

If you continue to allow your flesh to dominate you, you will continue to miss it. If you continue to let your natural mind dominate you, and do not get your mind renewed with the Word, you will continue to miss it.

That's why Paul wrote born-again, Spirit-filled Christians at Rome and told them to do two things: First, they were to present their bodies, and second, they were to renew their minds with the Word (Rom. 12:1,2).

Until your mind is renewed with the Word of God, your flesh and your unrenewed mind will dominate your spirit. That will keep you as a baby Christian — a carnal Christian.

Paul said to the church at Corinth, *"I, brethren, could not speak unto you as unto spiritual, but as unto carnal, even as unto babes in Christ"* (1 Cor. 3:1).

"For ye are yet carnal . . . ," he said (v. 3). One translation says, "For you are yet body-ruled."

Then he told them, *". . . and* [ye] *walk as men"* (v. 3). Another translation says, "Ye walk as mere men." What did he mean? He meant they were walking and doing things just like unsaved men do.

When you get your mind renewed with the Word, then your mind will side in with your spirit instead of with your body. And the two of them — your spirit through your mind — will control your body.

My spirit will not tell me something wrong. It has the nature of God in it; it has the life of God in it; it has the love of God in it; and it has the Spirit of God in it.

> **2 PETER 1:4**
> 4 Whereby are given unto us exceeding great and precious promises: that by these ye might be partakers of the divine nature. . . .

We are born of God. Then we feed on the Word of God. By so doing we are partakers of the divine nature, God's nature. If we have the divine nature in us, our spirit will not tell us to do something wrong.

Whatever your spirit tells you will be right.

Chapter 22
I Perceive

Now when much time was spent, and when sailing was now dangerous, because the fast was now already past, Paul admonished them, And said unto them, Sirs, I perceive that this voyage will be with hurt and much damage, not only of the lading and ship, but also of our lives.
— Acts 27:9,10

Paul said, "*I perceive. . . .*" He did not say, I have a revelation. He did not say, the Lord told me. He said, "I perceive."

How did he perceive it?

By the inward witness. He did not perceive it mentally. He did not perceive it physically. In his spirit he had this witness.

A family of seven had gone out to eat. The family had not been at the restaurant very long when the father suddenly said, "Let's go home."

"Why?"

"I don't know. I just have an urge, a perception, that we should."

They rushed home. A fire had started. If they had waited, everything would have burned. But the inward witness warned them in time.

If their home had burned down, someone might have said, "God did that. He had some purpose in it."

No, we have missed it because we haven't listened on the inside — in our spirits. We have not been spirit-conscious.

You cannot find anywhere in the Bible where God causes these things to happen to teach His people something. If those on that ship had listened to Paul, they

91

could have saved the ship and the merchandise. As it was, they lost everything and almost lost their lives. They would have lost their lives, too, if they had not started listening to Paul.

God is not an enemy! He is trying to help us! He is not working against us! He is working for us!

As we become more spirit-conscious we can learn how to better cooperate with Him.

Remember that the primary way God leads His children is by the inward witness.

Chapter 23
Spectacular Guidance

Whereupon, O king Agrippa, I was not dis-
obedient unto the heavenly vision. — Acts 26:19

God leads us today just like He led the first Christians. His Word works now just like it did then. It has not changed. The Spirit of God has not changed. God does not change.

The early believers did not have one Church back then, and we have another Church now. We have made a mistake in thinking that. We are in the same age they were in — the Church Age. We are in the same Church. We have the same Holy Spirit. It has seemed to us, however, that they had a whole lot we don't have. Not so.

"For as many as are led by the Spirit of God, they are the sons of God" (Rom 8:14). There are sons of God today. And the Spirit of God is still leading sons of God.

So we look into the Acts of the Apostles and elsewhere in the Bible to see how the Spirit of God led them. At times some received guidance through a vision. Others received guidance from an angel who appeared and told them what to do.

Such phenomena, however, did not happen every day in these people's lives. They occurred once or twice in a lifetime for most. So these are not the ordinary ways God leads. We get the impression that nearly every day an angel appeared to someone and told them something. That is not so.

Too many times while God is trying to bear witness with our spirit, trying to guide us the way He said He would in His Word, we do not listen because we want something such as a vision or an angel to appear.

We have no right to seek a vision. We have no right

to ask for an angel. There are no scriptures which say that we should. We do have a right to claim what the Bible promises. If God wants to send an angel, fine. If He wants to give a vision, fine.

As a young minister I did the same thing most Christians have done in the babyhood stage of their Christianity. I heard people talking about visions and angels, and I prayed something like that would happen to me. It never did.

Then I matured spiritually so that I never expected it to happen. I did not pray that it would happen. I did not expect it. But back in 1949, I was praying one day in the last church I pastored. I had shut myself up in the church to wait on God because I had a witness in my spirit that I should do so. Then the Holy Spirit — not my spirit — spoke to me.

Before I tell you what He said, look at the following passage of scripture with me and see how Peter saw a vision and then was led by the voice of the Spirit of God:

> ACTS 10:9-11
> 9 On the morrow, as they went on their journey, and drew up nigh unto the city, Peter went up upon the housetop to pray about the sixth hour:
> 10 And he became very hungry, and would have eaten: but while they made ready, he fell into a trance,
> 11 And saw heaven opened, and a certain vessel descending unto him, as it had been a great sheet knit at the four corners, and let down to the earth.

God showed Peter through a vision that He was going to bring in the Gentiles. Now we will skip to verse 19:

> ACTS 10:19,20
> 19 While Peter thought on the vision, THE SPIRIT SAID unto him, Behold, three men seek thee.
> 20 Arise therefore, and get thee down, and go with them, doubting nothing: for I have sent them.

These were three men from Cornelius' household. After Peter went to Cornelius' house in Caesarea and preached to these Gentiles, he went up to Jerusalem where the Bible says, "... *they that were of the circumcision contended with him*" (Acts 11:2). In Acts chapter 11, Peter is rehearsing what had happened to him in Acts chapter 10.

> ACTS 11:11,12
> 11 And, behold, immediately there were three men already come unto the house where I was, sent from Caesarea unto me.
> 12 AND THE SPIRIT BADE ME GO with them, nothing doubting. . . .

The Holy Spirit spoke to Peter. It may have been that Peter looked around to see who had spoken to him, I don't know. But he knew that the Spirit of God bade him go.

The Spirit spoke to me as I was waiting there in my church. The Holy Spirit said, "I am going to take you on to revelations and visions."

Immediately, revelations, in line with the Word — I'm not talking about something out of line with the Bible — began to come. Then in 1950 the visions began to come. Jesus Himself appeared to me and talked to me on various occasions. There were also other visions.

Chapter 24
The Spirit Bade Me Go

Now there were in the church that was at Antioch certain prophets and teachers; as Barnabas, and Simeon that was called Niger, and Lucius of Cyrene, and Manaen, which had been brought up with Herod the tetrarch, and Saul. As they ministered to the Lord, and fasted, THE HOLY GHOST SAID, Separate me Barnabas and Saul for the work whereunto I have called them.   — Acts 13:1,2

The Holy Ghost *said.* It would be of interest, first of all, to notice under what conditions the Holy Ghost said something. *"As they ministered to the Lord, and fasted, the Holy Ghost said. . . ."*

I am convinced we need to have services where we minister to the Lord. Too often we just minister to one another. Bible studies are good; we need them. Special singing is fine. But too many times we are not singing to the Lord; we are singing to the congregation. Let's have some services where we minister to the Lord; where we wait on Him. In that kind of an atmosphere the Holy Ghost can speak to us.

This was a group of five ministers. I do not know how the Holy Ghost spoke to them. It could have been that one of the prophets spoke it out. Of this I am sure — they all heard and they all agreed that the Holy Ghost was talking.

The Holy Ghost said, *"Separate me Barnabas and Saul for the work whereunto I have called them"* (Acts 13:2).

Peter said, *". . . The Spirit bade me go . . ."* (Acts 11:12).

After I had been in the ministry many years, death came and fastened itself upon my body. I know when death comes; I have been dead twice and came back. I know how it feels. Actually, I started to fall into the arms of death, when the Spirit of God came on me and lifted me up.

I heard a Voice speak. To me it was audible. I believe it was Jesus. I know that it was the Holy Spirit speaking. We discussed earlier how the Holy Ghost speaks not of Himself, but whatever He hears, that shall He speak. So the Holy Spirit heard God or Jesus say this, and He repeated it.

It sounded like a man's voice. It said, "Thou shalt not die, but thou shalt live. I want you to go teach My people faith. I have taught you faith through My Word. I have permitted you to go through certain experiences. You have learned faith both through My Word and by experience. Now go teach My people what I have taught you. Go teach My people faith."

The moment that voice ceased speaking I was perfectly well.

I have endeavored to be obedient to that heavenly Voice. That is the reason I teach faith so much — I am supposed to do it.

I will refer again now to the time Jesus appeared to me in 1959 in El Paso, Texas. It was during this vision that He told me, "Go teach My people how to be led by My Spirit." I have been dilatory about this. But I am going to do more teaching on this from now on. This is the reason for this book.

Chapter 25
Guidance Through Prophecy

Follow after charity, and desire spiritual gifts,
but rather that ye may prophesy.
— 1 Corinthians 14.1

Are all apostles? are all prophets? are all
teachers? are all workers of miracles?
— 1 Corinthians 12:29

Paul, speaking to the elders of the church at Ephesus in his farewell message, said, *"And now, behold, I go bound in the spirit unto Jerusalem, not knowing the things that shall befall me there: Save that the Holy Ghost witnesseth in every city, saying that bonds and afflictions abide me"* (Acts 20:22,23).

Then in chapter 21, while on his journey Paul landed at Tyre where the ship was to be unladen. Luke, the writer of Acts, was with Paul. He wrote, *"And finding disciples, we tarried there seven days: who said to Paul through the Spirit, that he should not go up to Jerusalem"* (v.4).

Paul continued on his journey:

ACTS 21:8-14
8 And the next day we that were of Paul's company departed, and came unto Caesarea: and we entered into the house of Philip the evangelist, which was one of the seven; and abode with him.
9 And the same man had four daughters, virgins, which did prophesy.
10 And as we tarried there many days, there came down from Judaea a certain prophet, named Agabus.
11 And when he was come unto us, he took Paul's girdle, and bound his own hands and feet, and said, Thus saith the Holy Ghost, So shall the Jews at Jerusalem bind the man that owneth this girdle, and shall deliver him into the

hands of the Gentiles.
12 And when we heard these things, both we, and they of that
place, besought him not to go up to Jerusalem.
13 Then Paul answered, What mean ye to weep and to break
mine heart? for I am ready not to be bound only, but also to
die at Jerusalem for the name of the Lord Jesus.
14 And when he would not be persuaded, we ceased, saying,
The will of the Lord be done.

Some have thought that Paul missed it. However, when
Paul did go up to Jerusalem and was arrested, Jesus stood
by Paul in the night. He appeared to him in a vision. He
did not rebuke Paul. Jesus did not tell Paul that he had
missed it. He said, "... *Be of good cheer, Paul: for as thou
hast testified of me in Jerusalem, so must thou bear
witness also at Rome"* (Acts 23:11).

No, Paul did not miss it. What God was doing was
preparing Paul for what was ahead of him.

Notice that we have two different things operating
here: (1) the gift of prophecy; (2) the ministry of the
prophet. They are different. They are not the same. It is
a mistake to confuse the two, yet this is often done.

The fact that one prophesies does not make him a
prophet. The Word of God plainly teaches that everyone
should desire to prophesy (1 Cor. 14:1). However, if just
prophesying made you a prophet, then it would seem that
the Lord was saying that everyone should desire to be a
prophet. Yet Paul asked, *"Are all apostles? are all
prophets? . . ."* (1 Cor. 12:29). The answer is no. Since all
could not be prophets, God would not tell us to seek
something we could not have.

The simple gift of prophecy is speaking unto men to
edification and exhortation and comfort (1 Cor. 14:3).
Prophecy is a supernatural utterance in a known tongue —
your own tongue. (Speaking in tongues is supernatural
utterance in an unknown tongue — a tongue unknown to
you.) Prophecy can be used in prayer, as well as tongues.

Sometimes when you are prophesying, it seems as if there are two of you. It seems to me as if I am standing right beside myself. You see, it is coming from my inward man where the Spirit of God who is prophesying abides. I listen with my natural ears to see what He said.

The Office of the Prophet

There is the office of the prophet. Without going into detail about it, we will touch the office of the prophet briefly concerning guidance. For one to be a prophet, he stands in that office and uses that ministry. Other spiritual gifts besides prophecy must operate in his ministry. The simple gift of prophecy, as we have said, is for speaking unto men for edification, and exhortation, and comfort. In this simple gift of prophecy there is no *foretelling* — no prediction whatsoever. However, in the ministry of the prophet there is foretelling and prediction. A prophet has the revelation gifts (the word of wisdom, the word of knowledge, and/or the discerning of spirits) in operation along with prophecy.

It is important to realize that spiritual things can be misused just as natural things can be misused. Some folks have never realized that. They think that just because it is spiritual, it has to be perfect — that it cannot be misused.

I have known people who were at one time wealthy who are now bankrupt because they listened to someone prophesy how to invest their money.

I remember a dear man who was in one of my meetings. I knew who he was, but I didn't really know him. I did not know that he would never make a business deal without calling a so-called "prophet" to prophesy to him what to do.

I said to him, "I seem to be impressed to say this to

you. You are going to lose everything you have and go bankrupt if you keep listening to whoever is advising you."

He didn't listen. The poor fellow, who was very wealthy, lost his home and everything he had. I have seen this happen not just one time, but many times.

I have seen ministers who have lost their ministries because of wrong prophecies.

You have to judge prophecies by the Word of God. If prophecy is not in line with the Word of God, it is not right.

Secondly, you have to judge personal prophecies by what you have in your own spirit. If you do not have something in your own spirit, do not accept a personal prophecy.

For years I have traveled extensively in the ministry. Everywhere I go there is always someone who has a "word" from the Lord for me — sometimes two or three. In all these years only one or two of them have been correct.

Do not build your life on prophecies. Do not guide your life by prophecies. Build your life on the Word! Let those other things be secondary. Put the Word of God first!

People sometimes say, "Well, if God is doing it, it has to be all right."

You have to realize that it isn't exactly God doing it. It is men prophesying under the inspiration of the Spirit of God. Anything that man has to do with, is not perfect. The Spirit of God is perfect. The gifts of the Spirit in themselves are perfect. But they certainly are not always perfect in manifestation, because they are manifested through imperfect vessels. This is the reason prophecy and tongues with interpretation need to be judged by the Word.

1 CORINTHIANS 14:29,30
29 Let the prophets speak two or three, and let the other judge.

**30 If any thing be revealed to another that sitteth by, let
the first hold his peace.**

"Let the prophets speak. . . . " The Bible is talking about
prophets here — not just anyone who prophesies. Do not
accept something just because a prophet said it. It is to
be judged according to the Bible. We do not judge people.
We judge what was *said.*

Now notice verse 30. *"If any thing be revealed to
another* [prophet]. . . . " Prophets have revelations. Others
might occasionally, but prophets have a ministry along
this line.

1 CORINTHIANS 14:32
**32 And the spirits of the prophets are subject to the
prophets.**

Some have said, "God made me do that. I couldn't help
but say that." The spirits of the prophets are subject to
the prophets. That means a person does not *have* to say
it. It comes out of his spirit. It is subject to him. The gift
of tongues, the interpretation of tongues, and prophecy
operate under the unction of the Spirit. And it might be
that God through these methods would give us a word of
knowledge, a word of wisdom, or revelation as we need it.
But we initiate the operation of prophecy. We initiate the
operation of tongues and interpretation. We are the ones
who have to speak it out.

Many times when the Spirit of God is moving, anyone
who can prophesy could do so — but that does not mean
one should. Also, when the Spirit is in manifestation,
anyone who is used in the ministry gift of tongues and
interpretation could speak — but that does not mean he
should. Have that *unction* of the Spirit to do it — other-
wise just sit there and let God move through someone else
who has it.

I held a seven-week meeting in a church years ago.
Every single night about the same time, at the same spot
in the service, just as they got ready to pass the offering
plates, this woman got up and spoke with tongues. She
said the same thing in tongues every night. After a while
I could have said the same things she said. If no one else
would interpret it, she would. It was like someone poured
cold water over the crowd. It deadened the service.

The pastor asked me to teach the auditorium class one
Sunday morning when he had to be out of town. This was
unusual — but I finished before the bell rang. One of the
deacons said, "Brother Hagin, may I ask a question?"

"Well, yes," I said. I thought it would be in line with
the lesson.

He said, "When messages in tongues with interpretation are given in public assembly, shouldn't they be a blessing to the congregation? Should it kill the service?"

That dear woman was sitting right in front of me.

I said, "That is beside the lesson. I'd rather not get
into that right now."

But others, some of the leaders of the church, said,
"Brother Hagin, we ought to answer that."

So I said, "If it is in the Spirit, it will lift the service
high. It will not push it down."

That woman was intelligent enough to catch on to that.
She came to me and said, "I have been wrong, haven't I?"

I said, "Yes ma'am, you have."

She said, "I thought so all the time. There was a
witness on the inside of me that knew that. But I wanted
to be used of God. I am going to stop that."

I said, "Thank you. You are a real blessing to the
church."

Others might have gotten angry about it saying, "They
won't allow God to move."

Sometimes folks do speak out, like this woman, without

the unction of the Spirit. This does not do away with the fact that her tongues were real. However, they were in imperfect operation. They were misused.

I admonish people to be very careful about personal prophecies. So many lives have been shipwrecked and ruined by not being careful regarding personal prophecy. Don't marry someone because someone prophesied you should. I have seen many such so-called "prophecies" through the years. I have never seen one of those marriages work out yet. Homes have been broken up by so-called prophecies.

Also, don't go into the ministry because somebody prophesied you should. Get it on the inside of you for yourself. Then if a prophecy confirms what you already have, that's all right. Jesus said to me when He appeared in that vision in 1959, "If the prophecy confirms what you already have, accept it. If it does not, don't accept it."

The Holy Ghost said, *"Separate me Barnabas and Saul for the work whereunto I have called them"* (Acts 13:2). He had already called them. This was just a confirmation of it.

In the last church I pastored there was a certain young person who was beautiful spiritually. My wife said to me, "I believe the hand of the Lord is on him. God is calling him into the ministry."

I said, "I have that conviction myself. But I am not going to "call" anyone. I am not going to tell anyone they are called, even if I know they are."

This is why. When one gets out in the ministry, it isn't always easy. Paul told the young minister, Timothy, "Endure hardness as a good soldier" (2 Tim. 2:3). When the way gets hard — and it will — you can have the victory. But it will get hard and someone who is not convinced of the call for themselves may say, "I just went because Daddy said so." Or, "Someone prophesied to me; I really don't know that I am called." But one who makes that dedication from his own spirit, who knows God called him, will stand through hell or high water.

So I did not say anything to this young person. Then one Sunday night we were all praying around the altar. I went around and laid hands on people to pray as God would lead me. I stopped beside this young man who was kneeling in the altar in intense prayer. I opened my mouth to pray, but I heard these words come out, "This is a confirmation of what I said to you at 3 o'clock this afternoon as you were praying down in the storm cellar. You asked for a confirmation and this is it. That was Me speaking to you."

After the prayer service I asked, "Were you praying down in the storm cellar at 3 o'clock this afternoon?"

(I wanted to check up — if I am wrong, I want to get right. If I miss it, I just admit, "I missed it." Don't be afraid to say, "I missed it." When I first started learning to drive a car I missed it a few times and ran up over the curb. But I didn't quit driving just because I missed it. Did you? We ought to have as much sense about spiritual things. Just because I missed it, I am not going to quit. I am going to keep going. I will just see to it that I don't miss it again. So I was checking up on it to see.)

This young person said, "Yes, I was praying. You know, Brother Hagin, I have felt for some time that God had a call on my life, but I didn't say yes or no. So I was spending time down in the cellar (which was fixed up like a nice basement) praying, meditating, reading the Bible, waiting on God. I felt that the Lord spoke to me and said, 'I have called you to the ministry — and I will confirm it tonight in the service.' But I didn't know how He would."

Remember — if it does not bear witness, or confirm something you already have, do not accept a personal prophecy.

As long as the gift of prophecy stays in the realm of speaking to men for edification, exhortation, and comfort, it is wonderful. Encourage that. But many times someone who prophesies may see a prophet minister with a word of foreknowledge. Then he begins to think, "I prophesy, so I can do that." Then he moves out of the place where he should be, into the other realm where he should not be.

A woman came up to me in one of our seminars we held in Tulsa. She had come with a group from a nearby city. She said, "Brother Hagin, this is all new to us. In our town we have a weekly prayer group. I want to ask you something about it. Some of them think I am wrong, but I don't think what we are doing is right. Actually, I don't know if I would call it a prayer meeting — all they ever do is lay hands on one another and prophesy. They spend all afternoon prophesying over one another. And I don't ever get anything but a bad prophecy.

"They prophesied that my mother was going to die within six months. That was eighteen months ago and she is not dead. Then they prophesied that my husband was going to leave me. He's not saved but he is a fine man and I love him. He is a good provider. We don't have any trouble. Those are just two examples. I always get prophecies that something bad is going to happen — but nothing bad has ever happened."

I said, "No, and it won't either. You are a child of God."

She said, "Isn't that a misuse?"

I said, "Yes, it is."

We need to know these things. It is very easy for babies to be misled and misguided. We can get off track. That's why Paul wrote to the church at Corinth about these things.

Chapter 26
Guidance Through
Visions

*There was a certain man in Caesarea called
Cornelius, a centurion of the band called the
Italian band, a devout man, and one that feared
God with all his house, which gave much alms
to the people, and prayed to God alway. He saw
in a vision evidently about the ninth hour of the
day an angel of God coming in to him, and saying unto him. . . .* — Acts 10:1-3

Sometimes God leads through visions.

Cornelius was a devout man, but he was not born again.
He did not know about Jesus. He was a Jewish proselyte.
The angel who appeared to him in this vision could not
preach the gospel to him. God did not call angels to preach
the gospel; God called men to preach the gospel. However,
the angel did tell Cornelius where to send for someone who
could preach the gospel to him and tell him how to be
saved.

Cornelius saw an angel in a vision. Angels also have
the ability, as God permits, to take upon themselves a
visible form which can be seen with the natural eye, just
as you can see a physical person.

HEBREWS 13:2
2 Be not forgetful to entertain strangers: for thereby some
have entertained angels unawares.

The scripture calls Cornelius' experience a vision
(Acts 10:3). It was a spiritual vision. Cornelius saw into
the spirit world, and there are angels out there in the spirit
world. If others had been present, they would not have

seen anything. Yet if the angel had taken on a visible form, anyone could have seen it.

There are three kinds of visions: spiritual visions, trances, and open visions.

In a spiritual vision, you see with the eyes of your spirit — not with your physical eye. When Paul saw the Lord in Acts 9, it was a spiritual vision. He did not see Him with his physical eyes.

> **ACTS 9:8**
> 8 And Saul arose from the earth; and when his eyes were opened, he saw no man: but they led him by the hand, and brought him into Damascus.

When the Lord spoke to Saul, his eyes were shut. Therefore, whatever it was that Paul saw, he did not see it with his physical eyes. We know this because the Bible says that when his eyes WERE OPENED, he was blind.

The second type of vision is when one falls into a trance. Cornelius did not fall into a trance — but Peter did.

> **ACTS 10:9-11**
> 9 On the morrow, as they went on their journey, and drew nigh unto the city, Peter went up upon the housetop to pray about the sixth hour:
> 10 And he became very hungry, and would have eaten: but while they made ready, he fell into a trance,
> 11 And saw heaven opened, and a certain vessel descending unto him, as it had been a great sheet knit at the four corners, and let down to the earth.

When one falls into a trance, his physical senses are suspended. He does not know where he is right at the moment. He is not unconscious, but he does not know what is going on around him. He is more conscious of spiritual things than physical things.

The third type of vision is what I call an open vision. The vision that occurred in El Paso in 1959 (which I have referred to in this book), was an open vision. My eyes were wide open. My physical senses were intact. I did not fall into a trance. Jesus walked into my room. I saw Him with my physical eyes.

Of all the visions I have had, only two were open visions. Three of them occurred when I fell into a trance. The rest were spiritual visions.

There were different types of visions in the Acts of the Apostles. There are different types of visions now.

For example, in visions, sometimes things are symbolic. In Peter's vision they were. He saw all manner of creeping things, both clean and unclean. He had to think on the vision in order to understand it (Acts 10:19). The Spirit spoke to him as he thought upon the vision and bade him go with three men to Cornelius' house. Peter still didn't know exactly what the vision meant. But when he went, things happened, and he began to understand that God had called the Gentiles into redemption as well as the Jews.

> ACTS 8:26-29
> 26 And the angel of the Lord spake unto Philip, saying, Arise, and go toward the south unto the way that goeth down from Jerusalem unto Gaza, which is desert.
> 27 And he arose and went: and, behold, a man of Ethiopia, an eunuch of great authority under Candace queen of the Ethiopians, who had the charge of all her treasure, and had come to Jerusalem for to worship,
> 28 Was returning, and sitting in his chariot read Esaias the prophet.
> 29 Then the Spirit said unto Philip, Go near, and join thyself to this chariot.

Some church people admit that God spoke to the apostles such as Peter, but they say that such divine visitations were only for the apostles. But Philip was not an apostle. He was elected as a deacon first (Acts 6:5). The highest office he ever filled was that of the evangelist

(Acts 21:8). Isn't it sad that in the church world we have
been robbed of the blessings and the supernatural
manifestations we should have had because people closed
the book on the supernatural and said, "That was just for
the apostles. All that ceased when the apostles of the New
Testament died."

ACTS 9:10-12
10 And there was a certain disciple at Damascus, named
Ananias; and to him said the Lord in a vision, Ananias. And
he said, Behold, I am here, Lord.
11 And the Lord said unto him, Arise, and go into the
street which is called Straight, and enquire in the house
of Judas for one called Saul of Tarsus: for, behold, he
prayeth,
12 And hath seen in a vision a man named Ananias coming
in, and putting his hand on him, that he might receive his
sight.

Ananias was not a deacon. He was just a disciple. He
was what we would call a layman. Yet the Lord used him.
We should all put ourselves in a position where God can
use us as He sees fit. We don't have to wait for a vision
before we do something for God. God may give us a vision,
or He may not. An angel may appear to us, or one may not.

It was a great privilege for me to speak in the church
of a certain great man of God when he was past seventy
years of age. He had been filled with the Spirit way back
at the turn of the century and had gone out to China as
a missionary in 1912. He told me of many marvelous
experiences he'd had.

He had a Bible study every Friday night in his church.
(I believe he was one of the world's foremost Bible
teachers — and I have heard most of them.) He related
this to me: He said he would teach certain subjects as the
Lord directed, but he also let the congregation suggest
subjects by writing them down on a slip of paper. On one

occasion, the majority of the congregation wrote, "We would like some teaching on angels. We have never heard any teaching on that subject."

He had spent a number of years teaching in one of the best Pentecostal Bible schools, and he thought he could cover the subject in two weeks. But he said, "The more I studied, the bigger it got. I taught six weeks and still did not cover the subject."

This man was an official of his Full Gospel denomination. Soon after this teaching on angels he was in a business meeting with leaders of that denomination. One matter of discussion concerned the report that a minister of their denomination claimed to have seen an angel. He said that the angel instructed him concerning his ministry. They were about to bar him from the denomination.

This Bible teacher said, "I just sat there and listened. I didn't even comment. I never did talk unless I was called on to talk. I could see the trend; they were about ready to turn this other minister out of the denomination."

Finally, one brother got up and said, "I believe we ought to hear from Brother S. He has been with us from the beginning of the movement. He is one of our most able Bible teachers. Let's hear what he has to say."

He told me he began by telling them about the study of angels he had just completed and taught in his church. Then he said, "I am not the least bit concerned because one out of several thousand of our ministers has seen an angel. The thing that disturbs me is why more of us are not seeing them.

"Then secondly," he told them, "if we are going to turn this man out for seeing an angel who instructed him concerning his ministry, what are we going to give our people in the place of it? Do we have anything better? anything more supernatural? anything more Scriptural? If we do not, I think we had better stay with what we have."

Quickly, someone jumped to his feet and said, "I move that we table this and forget all about it." They voted unanimously to leave it alone.

In 1963, my office occupied only the den of my little frame home in Garland, Texas. It wasn't really much of an office at that. Some men in another city contacted me. They said, "If you will move your office to this city, we will set up an office for you. We will buy all the office equipment, hire the secretaries, and pay their salaries. You won't have to pay anything. Let's get some of your material published."

Another man, who was an electronic technician, said, "Brother Hagin, if you will let me, I will make tapes of all your sermons. It won't cost you a thing. I will furnish all the materials free of charge."

Those offers sounded good. You would think God must be in them. But about that time I was praying with a certain group. We were having special times of ministering to the Lord. It was the kind of atmosphere Acts 13:1 and 2 speaks of — an atmosphere where God will move.

I was sitting on the platform beside a chair, praying, when suddenly Jesus stood right in front of me. I had my eyes shut. It was a spiritual vision. I did not fall into a trance. Standing right behind Jesus, about two feet to His right and three feet behind Him, was a large angel. I had seen angels before — but never one that big. He must have been 8 feet tall or more.

Jesus talked to me about some things. (And everything He said came to pass.) Occasionally, while He talked, I would glance at that angel. When I did, the angel would open his mouth and start to say something. When I looked back to Jesus, he would not say anything.

After Jesus finished His conversation with me, I asked, "Who is that fellow? What does he represent?"

Jesus said, "That's your angel."

I said, "My angel?"

"Yes," He said, "your angel. You read in the scriptures that I said concerning the little children that their angel is ever before My Father's face. You don't lose your angel just because you grow up."

(Isn't that comforting! I have that big fellow following me around. Praise the Lord!)

I said, "What does he want?"

Jesus said, "He has a message for you."

Then I got so letter-of-the-Word conscious I could have missed the Spirit. I said, "You are talking to me; why don't You give me the message? Why do I have to listen to an angel? Besides that, the Word of God says as many as are led by the Spirit of God, they are the sons of God. I have the Holy Ghost. Why couldn't the Holy Ghost talk to me?"

Jesus had mercy on me, and patience with me. He said, "Did you ever read in My Word where the angel of the Lord told Philip to go down to the way of Gaza? Wasn't that direction? Wasn't that guidance? Didn't my angel appear to Cornelius, and he wasn't even a born-again man? Didn't the angel tell him what to do?"

He gave me several more New Testament examples.

Finally, I said, "That's enough. I will listen." Then I looked up to this big fellow and said, "What is it?"

He started this way, "I am sent from the Presence of Almighty God to tell you not to let these men (and he called their names) set up an office for you. They have an ulterior motive. They will control your ministry because they will have put in all the money."

Then he called the name of the man who was the radio and electronic technician and said, "Don't let him have any of your tapes. He has an ulterior motive. If he gets them into his hands, he will control them. I am sent from the Presence of Almighty God to tell you that.

"Then I am sent from the Presence of Almighty God to tell you this: The money will come so that you can set up your own office, have your own books, have your own tapes. You will be the head of it, the sole boss, because I am going to tell you what to do, and not some man. Within four months, after everything is paid and cleared out, you will have enough money to get you headed this direction. For I have sent my angels out to cause the money to come."

When that time came, I had $4,000 which was enough to do what the Lord had told me to do. That was the beginning of this ministry.

I could tell more, but this is enough to illustrate that these things do happen. But let me emphasize this — although God does lead us through visions and other supernatural manifestations, I would encourage you NOT to seek a vision. You could get beyond the Word where the devil can deceive you. We often prefer to have a more direct word of guidance, but we don't always have it. So don't try to manufacture it, if it is not there. Nowhere in the Bible does it say that anyone was seeking a vision when one came. Visions just happened without anyone in the Bible seeking them.

Be content, if it is all you ever have, to follow the inward witness. But educate and train and develop your human spirit so that inward witness becomes more and more real to you.

Then, if God sees fit for supernatural visitations and manifestations, just thank God for them.

Know that the angels of God are with you. Your angel is with you whether you ever see him or not.

Chapter 27
Listen to Your Heart

Now when much time was spent, and when sailing was now dangerous, because the fast was now already past, Paul admonished them, And said unto them, Sirs, I PERCEIVE that this voyage will be with hurt and much damage, not only of the lading and ship, but also of our lives.
— Acts 27:9,10

Paul did not say, "The Lord told me" that this voyage will be with much hurt and damage. He simply said, "I *perceive*" that it will. In his spirit, Paul had an inward perception, an inward premonition, an inward witness that the voyage would be dangerous. This is the primary way God leads all of us.

Paul did not perceive it *mentally*. He did not have some kind of "vibration" or psychic experience. I don't like this "vibration" business. Spiritual perceptions are not in the psychic realm. You do not find psychic phenomenon in the Bible. Also, Paul did not perceive this *physically*. In his *spirit* he had a witness.

That belongs to all of us. The Holy Spirit abiding in our spirits must communicate with us through our spirits — not through our minds. That is why your spirit knows things your head doesn't know. But we have not been taught to listen to our spirits. And sometimes we are reluctant to do so.

The reason that we as Spirit-filled believers continually miss it, make mistakes, and fail is because our spirits, which should guide us, are kept locked away in prison, so to speak. Knowledge, or intellect, has taken the throne.

Any person who shuts his spirit away and never listens to it — because the spirit of man is the candle of the

117

Lord — becomes crippled in life and becomes an easy prey to selfish and designing people.

My wife and I held a meeting for a certain lady pastor — a very spiritually beautiful woman — who related this story to me herself:

An evangelist was coming to town. He got all the churches he could to cooperate with him in a city-wide meeting. He rented the city auditorium. It is a sorry thing to have to say, but everyone in the ministry is not honest. Because this man had a poor credit rating, the city auditorium demanded payment in advance. So he went through this woman pastor. She was gullible enough to say her church would stand responsible for $3,000 rent and all newspaper advertising. Crowds of 2,000 to 3,000 attended every night. He took up a lot of money, but he left town without paying one bill. This woman's church had to take $5,000 out of their building fund to cover this evangelist's expenses.

This lady pastor told me, "Brother Hagin, if I had listened to my heart, I would never have done that."

I said to her, "I heard you recovered your money."

She said, "I sure did. I found out where he was holding a meeting in another state. I got an airplane ticket and went there. The service had already started. I waited. Just when they were about to turn the service to him I marched down the aisle and toward the platform. An usher tried to stop me. I said, 'No, I am a minister of the gospel. I want to see this scoundrel.' I walked right up on the platform and plopped myself down beside him.

"I said, 'I have come after my $5,000. I will take the offering tonight. I brought my attaché case along. We will dump all the offering in there. And I will stay around here every night until my church recovers all of our money.'

"He said, 'Well, now we . . .'

"I said, 'No, if you don't give me back all of my money,

when they say they are going to turn the service over to you, I am going to take the pulpit and tell the people what happened. And not only that, I am going to follow you from meeting to meeting. In every meeting, I am going to come up on the platform and make the same announcement and tell the people what you did.' "

Needless to say, in two nights she had her money and she was on her way home. I glory in her spunk.

But the point I want to make is this. She said to me, "Brother Hagin, if I had listened to my spirit, this never would have happened. I don't mean if I had listened to a voice; I don't even mean a still, small voice. I just mean if I had listened to the inward witness. I had a check in my spirit. If I had listened to it, I wouldn't have stood good for his debts."

If we as individuals would have listened to our hearts — to an inward witness, or an inward voice — we would not have done some things we did.

I have lost money by not listening to that inward witness. I knew on the inside that I should not do some things. Why did I do it? Well, why do any of us not listen to the inward witness?

But just because you make a mistake, don't quit. You don't quit physically just because you make a mistake. If the phone rings in the middle of the night and you stumble over a stool and fall down trying to answer it, you don't just lie there. You get up and answer the phone. Just because you bust your shins or stub your toe physically, you don't quit. And just because you bust your shins or stub your toe spiritually, you don't quit either.

As I said, the person who keeps his spirit shut away and never listens to it becomes crippled in life. The person who listens to his spirit is the man or woman, boy or girl who climbs to the top!

If Christians would just check up on the inside of them,

in most of the affairs of life, they would know what to do.

You do not need to seek guidance when the Bible has already told you what to do. Go ahead and do it. The Bible tells you how to act in every circumstance of life. It tells husbands how to treat wives. It tells wives how to treat husbands. It tells parents how to treat their children. It tells children how to respond to their parents. The Bible tells all of us to walk in love — divine love. And that divine love, which seeks not its own, is also a matter of the heart.

Chapter 28
How To Train The Human Spirit

The spirit of man is the candle of the Lord. . . .
— Proverbs 20:27

The Lord enlightens us and guides us through our spirits. If that be the case — and it is — then we need to become more spirit-conscious. We need to become more conscious of the fact that we are spirit beings, and not just mental or physical beings. We need to train our spirits so they will become safer and safer guides.

One thing which has held back the Christian world as a whole is that we are more physical-conscious (body-conscious) and more mental-conscious (soul-conscious) than we are spirit-conscious. We have developed the body and the soul, but we have left the spirit of man almost untouched.

I have a cassette teaching tape which has helped many Christians in this area. In one of our meetings, one young man I know quite well gave his testimony of how it had helped him:

Just a few years ago, when he was 31 or 32, he went into business. He left his salaried job with a total of $5,500. He was single at that time and he had to use this money for living expenses as well as for capital. At one point, his nest egg dwindled to $50.

He gave this testimony: "I listened to Brother Hagin's tapes. There were three on faith and confession, and one called "How To Train the Human Spirit." I went to bed every night listening to that tape. I put it on in the morning and listened to it while I shaved. I listened to it over and over and over again — probably hundreds of times — until that message got into my spirit. Then by listening to my spirit and using my faith, my assets now total in excess of $30 million."

This young man is only about 38 years old now. He is not a preacher. He is a businessman. He has told me how his spirit has spoken to him and told him how to invest and buy land.

I will give the essence of the teaching contained on that cassette in this chapter: How To Train the Human Spirit.

Your spirit can be educated just as your mind can be educated. Your spirit can be built up in strength and trained just as your body can be built and trained. Here are four rules by which you can train and develop your own human spirit.

1. By meditation in the Word
2. By practicing the Word
3. By giving the Word first place
4. By instantly obeying the voice of your spirit

1. *BY MEDITATION IN THE WORD OF GOD*

The most deeply spiritual men and women I know are those who give time to meditation in the Word of God. You cannot develop spiritual wisdom without meditation. God made that fact known to Joshua just after the death of Moses at the very beginning of Joshua's ministry.

> **JOSHUA 1:8**
> 8 This book of the law shall not depart out of thy mouth; but thou shalt meditate therein day and night, that thou mayest observe to do according to all that is written therein: for then thou shalt make thy way prosperous, and then thou shalt have good success.

If God did not want Joshua to be prosperous, why did He tell him how to prosper? If He did not want him to succeed, why did He tell him how to have good success? He wanted Joshua to be successful — and He wants you to be successful.

Paraphrasing this truth in New Testament language, we would say, "The Word of God — particularly the New Testament — shall not depart out of your mouth. But meditate therein day and night, that you may observe to do according to all that is written therein: for then you will make your way prosperous and you will have good success."

If you ever want to do anything great in life, if you ever want to amount to anything in life, *take time to meditate in the Word of God.* Start out with at least 10 or 15 minutes a day — then increase the time.

I left the last church I pastored in 1949 and I have been out in the field ministry ever since. I used to do much more fasting and a different kind of praying than I do now. (You learn things as you go along.) Running two services a day — which I always did — and sometimes three, takes a lot out of you physically as well as spiritually. I would teach every morning, pray out loud all afternoon, and preach every night. I ate only one meal a day during my meetings and by exerting so much physical energy, I would grow weak. Then two days a week were my fast days — Tuesday and Thursday. I ate no food and drank no water for 24 hours.

One day the Lord said to me, "I would rather you would live a fasted life instead of having days and periods of fasting."

I said, "What do you mean? I never heard anyone say that!"

The Lord said, "Instead of having certain days you fast and then going back and eating all you want, just live a fasted life. Fasting does not change me anyhow. I am the same before you fast, while you fast, and when you get through fasting. It does not change My Word. It helps you keep your flesh under. So just don't ever eat all you want. Just keep your flesh under all the time."

Then He said, "Don't spend all that time in the afternoon praying and wearing yourself out before the night service. Lie on the bed and meditate."

So I began to lie there in the afternoons, meditating. And I got further meditating than I ever did praying and fasting. I grew more spiritually.

That is what God is saying in Joshua 1:8: "*. . . for then thou shalt make thy way prosperous. . . .*" I wanted to be prosperous in the ministry. "*. . . and then thou shalt have good success. . . .*" I wanted to have good success in the ministry. This works whether you are in the ministry, whether you raise cattle, sell automobiles, or whatever you do.

This Word of God shall not depart out of thy mouth. Talk about the Word. *But thou shalt meditate therein.* Think on the Word.

The Hebrew word translated *meditate* also carries this thought with it: *To mutter.* Mutter the Word. Speak it to yourself.

The Lord led me, before I ever heard anyone teach on meditation, to lie on the bed and mutter the Word. I just said it to myself. And I would have some of the most tremendous services. I developed myself spiritually, and at the same time conserved my physical strength.

I like another translation of Joshua 1:8. The last phrase reads like this: ". . . you shall be able to deal wisely in the affairs of life." You could not have good success if you did not know how to deal wisely in the affairs of life.

How can you know how to deal wisely in the affairs of life? Because you meditated in the Word of God and walked in the light of that Word.

2. *PRACTICING THE WORD*

Practicing the Word means being a doer of the Word.

JAMES 1:22
22 But be ye doers of the word, and not hearers only. . . .

We have many "talkers about the Word," and even many "rejoicers about the Word," but we do not have many "doers of the Word."

Begin to practice being a doer of the Word by doing in all circumstances what the Word tells you to do.

Some have thought that being a doer of the Word meant to keep the Ten Commandments. That is not what James 1:22 means. After all, under the New Covenant we have but one commandment — the commandment of love. Jesus said, *"A new commandment I give unto you, That ye love one another; as I have loved you, that ye also love one another"* (John 13:34).

A doer of the Word will do that. If you love someone, you won't steal from him. You won't lie about him. The New Testament says that love is the fulfilling of the law. If you walk in love you won't break any law which was given to curb sin.

Being a doer of the Word means that we are to do primarily what is written in the Epistles. They are the letters written to us, the Church. As an example of doing the Word, let us look at some instructions given us in one of the Epistles.

PHILIPPIANS 4:6
6 Be careful for nothing; but in every thing by prayer and supplication with thanksgiving let your requests be made known unto God.

So do that! Now we don't mind practicing part of this verse — the part that says to pray. But if you practice just that part and not the first part, you are not practicing the Word — you are not a doer of the Word.

The Amplified translation of Philippians 4:6 begins,

"Do not fret or have any anxiety about anything. . . ."
First we are told not to fret. If you are going to fret and
have anxieties, it will do no good to make requests. That
kind of praying does not work. An over-anxious prayer
full of fretfulness does not work.

I felt very sorry for a minister who came to me some
years ago. (But sometimes it doesn't give a man the answer
just to sympathize with him.) His life was full of storms
and tests. His stomach was upset; he couldn't keep down
what he ate. He couldn't sleep. His nerves were shot
because of a particular incident.

He came to me for help. I began to tell him what the
Word said and how to pray about this circumstance. When
I encouraged him to take this scripture and *do it,* he
rebelled. He said, "Oh, yes, but everyone doesn't have the
faith that you have."

I told him it was not a matter of having a lot of faith,
but a matter of endeavoring to practice the Word. I told
him if he would practice the Word, his faith would be built
up. And I told him how I practice this particular verse.

When I get alone, I read this verse aloud and I tell the
Lord that His Word is true and that I believe it.

I told this minister that he would be tempted to say
he couldn't help worrying and fretting. But that God had
not asked us to do something we cannot do. When God
said not to fret — that means we can keep from fretting
and being anxious. God is a just God and He will not ask
us to do something we cannot do.

When I first began practicing this verse it was easy
to believe that I could make my requests known unto
God — but it was hard to believe that I could *not fret.*
However, since God says we don't have to fret, then I
would say, "I refuse to fret or have any anxiety about
anything."

I tell the Lord that I bring my requests unto Him. Then

I thank Him for the answer. This quiets my spirit and pacifies the troubled spirit the devil tries to make me have.

Then I would go about my business. Before I knew it, however, the devil was trying to get me to fret again. I would simply go right back and read this verse again and keep claiming it.

This minister began to practice Philippians 4:6. He told me later that the problem worked out and did not get as big as he was expecting. He was about to be sued over a certain matter, but God helped him out of it.

It is possible to become so fretful over something that you cannot eat or sleep. But all you have to do is practice the Word and you will get results.

Philippians 4:7 is a result of practicing Philippians 4:6.

PHILIPPIANS 4:7
7 And the peace of God, which passeth all understanding, shall keep your hearts and minds through Christ Jesus.

Many people want what verse 7 talks about — but they don't want to practice what verse 6 says to do to get it. *The Amplified* translation of verse 7 says, "And God's peace . . . which transcends all understanding, shall garrison and mount guard over your hearts and minds in Christ Jesus." God's peace will keep guard over your heart and your mind.

But can you reap these results and have this peace without being a doer of the Word? No, you really cannot.

Verse 6 tells us not to fret. People who worry and fret, continually think on the wrong side of life. Verse 8 tells us what we are to think about.

PHILIPPIANS 4:8
8 Finally, brethren, whatsoever things are true, whatsoever things are honest, whatsoever things are just, whatsoever things are pure, whatsoever things are lovely, whatsoever things are of good report; if there be any virtue, and if there be any praise, think on these things.

DO verse 8. *Practice* this verse. Think about the right things. Many people think about the wrong things. You know what they think about because of what they talk about. The Bible says, ". . . out of the abundance of the heart, the mouth speaketh" (Matt. 12:34). They continually worry and fret and think on the wrong side of life — and they continually talk unbelief. You cannot be a doer of the Word and continue to talk unbelief. The more you talk about some things, the bigger they get. If something does not meet all of these qualifications — if it is not true, honest, just, pure, lovely, of good report — do not think about it and do not talk about it!

The Amplified translation of First Corinthians 13:7 reads, "Love . . . is ever ready to believe the best of every person." I have found through the years that most of the stories I have heard about people do not even meet the first qualification. They are not even true. So don't talk about the stories you hear. Don't even think about them. Some things you hear might even be true — but they might not be pure and lovely, and notice this — of a good report. Therefore we are not to think about them.

By thinking about such things, we give place to the devil. His greatest weapon is the power of suggestion. He is ever endeavoring to enter your thought life. That is why we are told in God's Word to, ". . . *think on these things.*"

Particularly in the Epistles, God the Holy Spirit is speaking to the Church. So meditate on these letters and what He has to say — and be a doer of the Word. You will grow spiritually.

3. *GIVE THE WORD FIRST PLACE*

The training, the developing, the educating of our spirits comes by giving the Word of God first place in our lives.

PROVERBS 4:20-22
20 My son, attend to my words; incline thine ear unto my sayings.

21 Let them not depart from thine eyes; keep them in the
midst of thine heart.
22 For they are life unto those that find them, and health
to all their flesh.

God says in this passage, "... *Attend to my words*
[Give heed to them — Put them first]; *incline thine ear unto
my sayings* [Listen to what I have to say]. *Let them not
depart from thine eyes* [Keep looking at the Word of God];
keep them [my Words] *in ... your heart."*

There are rich dividends for doing this. Why is it that
God tells us to put His Word first, and to listen to what
He has to say, to keep looking at His Word, and to keep
His Word in our heart? It is because "... *they* [His Words]
*are LIFE unto those that find them, and HEALTH to all
their flesh."*

The margin of the King James says the word translated
health is the Hebrew word for *medicine.* God's Word is
"medicine to all their flesh." There is healing in the Word.

In the twelve years I pastored, there were church
members who would get sick, go to the hopsital, and then
ask for prayer. I am not saying it is wrong to have a doctor,
certainly not. We believe in hospitals and doctors. Thank
God for them. But I am saying, why not put God's Word
first? Sometimes as a last resort, Christians will turn to
the Word.

A Baptist minister, who didn't even particularly believe
in divine healing at the time, told of how he'd had problems
with his tonsils. His doctor kept insisting that they be
removed. So the date was finally set for his tonsils to be
removed.

It was his family's custom to read the Bible and pray
together each morning before the children went to school.
On the very day this minister was scheduled to enter the
hospital, this family's daily scripture passage was the one

which tells of King Asa, who got a disease in his feet and instead of seeking the Lord, he sought physicians and he died (2 Chron. 16:12,13).

The minister said he was struck by this. He realized that he had not even prayed about his tonsils. He shared this with his wife and children and asked that they pray together about his tonsils.

When they prayed, the Lord told him not to have them removed. To his astonishment, the Lord healed the tonsils and he has had no more trouble with them.

There is a lesson to be learned here. The Bible does not imply that King Asa died because he put the physicians first. However, it does imply that he should have put the Lord first. We should train ourselves to put the Lord first.

We should train ourselves to ask ourselves concerning any matter, "What does God's Word have to say about this?" We should ask ourselves what God has to say about anything that may come up in our life — and then put that Word first.

Sometimes family and friends will try to rush you into things — but you need to think about what the Word of God says. Put God's Word first in every area of life.

4. *INSTANTLY OBEY THE VOICE OF YOUR SPIRIT*

The human spirit has a voice. We call that voice *conscience.* Sometimes we call it *intuition,* an *inner voice,* or *guidance.* The world calls it a *hunch.* But what it is, is your spirit speaking to you. Every man's spirit, saved or unsaved, has a voice.

The human spirit, as we have seen in previous chapters, is a spiritual man, a spirit man, an inward hidden man. He is hidden to the physical senses. You cannot see him with the physical eyes, nor touch him with your physical hands. This is the man who has become a new creature in Christ (2 Cor. 5:17). When a man is born again, his spirit becomes a new spirit.

God prophesied through both Ezekiel and Jeremiah that a time would come when He would take the old stony heart out of men and put in a new one. He said that He would put His Spirit into us. Under the New Covenant, this new birth became available.

The new birth is a rebirth of the human spirit. As Second Corinthians 5:17 tells us, if any man be in Christ, he is a new creature — everything that was old in his spirit, the old nature, is taken away, and all things have become new.

As you give this newborn spirit the privilege of meditating on the Word of God, the Word becomes the source of its information. Your spirit will become strong and the inward voice of your conscience, educated in the spirit, will become a true guide.

Did you notice that meditation in the Word, practicing the Word, giving the Word first place, all come before obeying your spirit? You see, if your spirit has had the privilege of meditating in the Word, of practicing the Word, of putting the Word first — then your spirit is an authoritative guide.

"The spirit of man is the candle of the Lord. . . ." (Prov. 20:27). Your newborn spirit has within it the life and nature of God. The Holy Spirit dwells within your spirit. *". . . greater is he that is in you, than he that is in the world"* (1 John 4:4). The Holy Spirit dwells in your spirit. God has to communicate with you through your spirit because that is where He is. Your spirit gets its information through Him.

Learn to obey the voice of your spirit.

If you are not accustomed to doing that, of course, you will not get there quickly. As we have said, your spirit can be built up and strengthened just as your body can be built up and strengthened. Your spirit can be educated just as your mind can be educated. But just as you did not begin school in the first grade one week and graduate from the twelfth grade the next week, your spirit will not be educated and trained overnight.

However, if you will follow these four points and practice them, after a while you can know the will of God the Father even in the minor details of life. You will receive guidance and will always instantly get either a *yes* or a *no*. You will know in your spirit what you should do in all the affairs of life.

Chapter 29
Praying in the Spirit

For if I pray in an unknown tongue, my spirit prayeth, but my understanding is unfruitful. What is it then? I will pray with the spirit, and I will pray with the understanding also: I will sing with the spirit, and I will sing with the understanding also. — 1 Corinthians 14:14,15

One of the greatest spiritual exercises there is, is to pray in tongues every single day. Your spirit is then in direct contact with the Father of spirits.

1 CORINTHIANS 14:2
2 For he that speaketh in an unknown tongue speaketh not unto men, but unto God: for no man understandeth him; howbeit in the spirit he speaketh mysteries.

It is your spirit praying when you pray in tongues — the Holy Ghost gives the utterance, but it is your spirit praying. Paul said, *"For if I pray in an unknown tongue, my spirit prayeth . . ."* (1 Cor. 14:14).

I have always followed the policy of daily praying in tongues. It keeps my spirit in contact with the Father of spirits. It helps me become more spirit-conscious.

When you pray in tongues, your mind grows quiet — because you are not praying out of your mind. And once your mind is quiet, you become more conscious of your own spirit, and of spiritual things.

Get out of the sense realm. Get out of the flesh realm. Get out of the human reasoning realm.

Get over into the faith realm and into the spirit realm. Faith is of the spirit — and that's where great things happen!

133

With millions of Faith Library books in circulation, the printed page continues to be a major outreach of Kenneth Hagin Ministries. The voice of Kenneth Hagin Ministries is further amplified around the world through the following media: A 24-page free monthly magazine, *The Word of Faith;* an international radio broadcast, "Faith Seminar of the Air"; nationwide All Faiths' Crusades; Faith Library tapes; and RHEMA Correspondence Bible School. These outreaches are vital to the part Kenneth Hagin Ministries shares in fulfilling the Great Commission — yet, there is more . . .

RHEMA Bible Training Center is another dynamic outreach of Kenneth Hagin Ministries. Founded in 1974, RHEMA offers a high quality of ministerial studies designed to train and equip men and women to enter the Evangelistic, Pastoral, Teaching, Missions, Helps, Youth, and Children's ministries. Today thousands of graduates of RHEMA have ventured into every inhabited continent of the earth, carrying the Good News of the Gospel of Jesus Christ — with signs following.

To receive a free, full-color brochure on RHEMA Bible Training Center, a free monthly magazine, *The Word of Faith,* or to receive our Faith Library Catalog with a complete listing of Kenneth Hagin Ministries' books and tapes, write:

Kenneth Hagin Ministries
P.O. Box 50126
Tulsa, OK 74150-0126

In Canada write:
P.O. Box 335, Islington (Toronto), Ontario, Canada, M9A 4X3

How You Can Be Led by the Spirit of God

In a vision many years ago, the Lord dealt with Kenneth E. Hagin about teaching His people how to be led by the Spirit of God. In recent years, the Lord has stirred Rev. Hagin up to teach more and more on this subject, and this highly acclaimed book is part of that stirring.

"Children of God can expect to be led by the Spirit of God," Rev. Hagin writes. "Many times, however, we seek guidance by means other than the way God said. When we do, we get into trouble."

This book has already helped many in the Body of Christ to be led by the Spirit. In it, Rev. Hagin gives step-by-step guidance through the Scriptures to steer Christians away from spiritual pitfalls and help them to follow the Spirit of God in every area of life. Among the subjects discussed are: "fleeces," the conscience, the inward witness, prophecy, visions, and training the human spirit.

About the Author

The ministry of Kenneth E. Hagin has spanned more than 50 years since God miraculously healed him of a deformed heart and incurable blood disease at the age of 17. Today the scope of Kenneth Hagin Ministries is worldwide. The ministry's radio program, "Faith Seminar of the Air," is heard coast-to-coast in the U.S., and reaches more than 80 nations. Other outreaches include: *The Word of Faith,* a free monthly magazine; All Faiths' Crusades, conducted nationwide; RHEMA Correspondence Bible School; RHEMA Bible Training Center; RHEMA Alumni Association and RHEMA Ministerial Association International; and a prison ministry outreach.

Kenneth Hagin Ministries

ISBN 0-89276-513-5